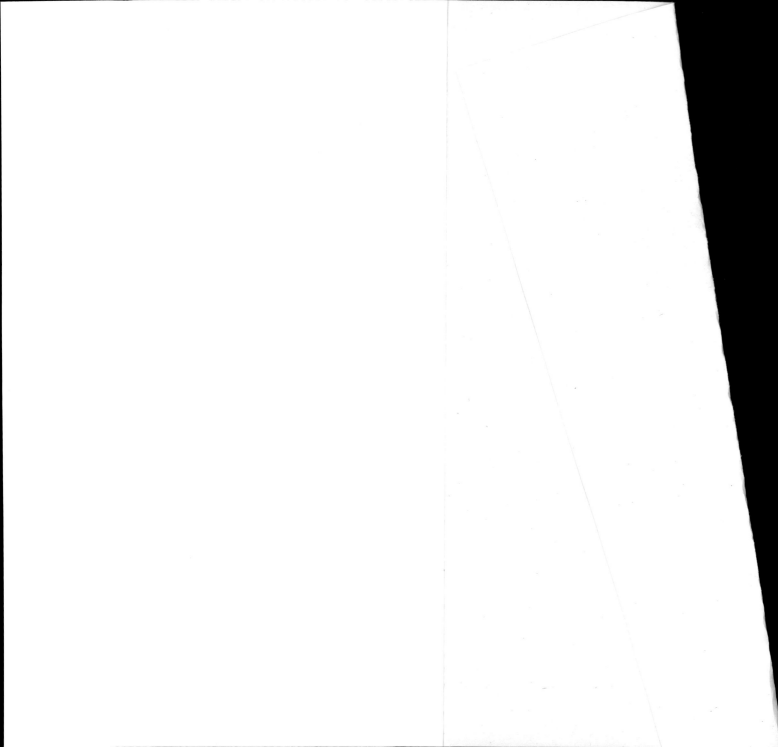

A
Parliament
of Owls

A Book of
Collective Nouns

CHLOE RHODES

Michael O'Mara Books Limited

This new edition first published in 2023
First published in Great Britain under the title *An Unkindness of Ravens*
in 2014 by
Michael O'Mara Books Limited
9 Lion Yard
Tremadoc Road
London SW4 7NQ

A CIP catalogue record for this book is available from the British Library.

Papers used by Michael O'Mara Books Limited are natural, recyclable
products made from wood grown in sustainable forests. The manufacturing
processes conform to the environmental regulations of the country of origin.

ISBN: 978-1-78929-595-5 in hardback print format
ISBN: 978-1-78243-317-0 in e-book format

1 2 3 4 5 6 7 8 9 10

Cover illustration by Chris Wormell
Illustrations by Aubrey Smith
Designed and typeset by Claire Cater
Cover Design by Ana Bjezancevic

Printed and bound by CPI Group (UK) Ltd, Croydon, CR0 4YY
www.mombooks.com

CONTENTS

For my rascal of boys, Matt, Stanley and Albert.

INTRODUCTION

Stand near woodland in early spring, after night has fallen and when the air is still, and if you're lucky, you'll hear the thrilling, trilling song of the nightingale. Perhaps you'll be luckier still and hear more than one; male nightingales sing to establish their territory and attract a mate, so if you're walking in a woodland after sunset you'll often hear several birds singing in harmony. It's hard to put into words such an ethereal experience, but if you tried, what would you say? What would you call a forest full of nightingales? These days we generally refer to most groups of birds as a flock. It's a practical, catch-all term that is usually adequate for conveying our meaning. But perhaps the timelessness of the nightingales' song has stirred something in you; you want to do justice to that proud, hopeful warbling.

You think of those half-remembered lines from John Keats' 'Ode to a Nightingale':

Thou wast not born for
death, immortal Bird!
No hungry generations
tread thee down;
The voice I hear this
passing night was heard
In ancient days by emperor and clown.

In the modern world, those ancient days can seem to belong to another universe. The pace of our lives, the speed of our technology, and the digitization of our human connections would all be unfathomable to our distant ancestors, just as their customs, cures and country lore can seem incomprehensible to us. But those nightingales singing in the twilight connect our two worlds. And so does the language that we use to describe them. In fact, the gradual evolution of our language over the centuries is a reminder that the past and the present are not two worlds but one. Many of the words English speakers use every day have their roots in the language used by the ancient civilizations and most of the sayings and idioms that form part of the lexicon of phrases we take for granted were already proverbial in the Middle Ages. One particularly rich stream of historically resonant language includes the words we use to describe groups of people, animals and

8

birds, properly known as collective nouns. If one of our fifteenth-century forefathers had witnessed that symphony of nocturnal bird song, he'd have said he'd heard 'a watch of nightingales'.

I love this as an example of a traditional collective noun because it is typical of the way a simple group name can provide a snapshot of the person, creature or thing it describes. A phenomenon American author James Lipton describes perfectly in his distinguished book on the subject, *An Exaltation of Larks*, as 'giving us large illuminations in small flashes'.

The aim of this book is to celebrate these nuggets of enlightenment, to explore their origins, set them in the social context in which they would first have been used and to attempt to share the view from the window that each one opens onto the medieval world. Why is a group of lions called a pride? Who called a flock of crows a murder? Why is a party of friars, or foxes, or thieves, referred to as a skulk?

Unusually for terms used in the Middle Ages, there is a paper trail to follow in pursuit of the origins of collective nouns. It's a trail that weaves and winds, more country lane than Roman road, but it is there, and this fact alone helps to explain where they came from. Unlike proverbs, rhymes or homilies, these terms were formally recorded because they formed part of the education of the nobility. In fact, they were created and perpetuated as a means of marking out the aristocracy from the less well-bred masses. Most of the traditional collective nouns we're aware of today – from a gaggle of geese to a kindle of kittens – appeared for the first time in fifteenth-century publications known as Books of Courtesy. These were handbooks on the various aspects of noble living designed to prepare young aristocrats for the formalities of their privileged lives and prevent them from embarrassing themselves or their families at court. Unless otherwise stated, all of the terms examined in this book can be traced back to these documents.

The earliest of these documents to survive to the present day was the Egerton Manuscript, dating from around 1450, which featured a list of 106 collective nouns. Several other manuscripts followed: two Harley Manuscripts, the Porkington Manuscript, the Digby Manuscript and the Robert of Gloucester Manuscript, each adding their own terms. Then, in 1476, William Caxton, who had just returned from Germany with the expertise to establish England's first printing press, published a version of John Lydgate's political poem 'Horse, Sheep and Goose'. On the final few pages, in keeping with the hand-written manuscripts that preceded it, he included a list of collective nouns. This was followed, in 1486, by the publication of the most influential of all the lists, which appeared in *The Book of St Albans*, a treatise on hunting, hawking and heraldry, written mostly in verse and attributed to the nun Dame Juliana Barnes (sometimes written Berners), prioress of the Priory of St Mary of Sopwell, near the town of St Albans.

Print historians have expressed uncertainty over the true identity of the book's author, but most seem content with the likelihood that Dame Juliana, who joined the convent from an aristocratic family, was responsible at least for the section on hunting, and for its accompanying list of group terms titled 'The companies of beasts and fowls'. This list features 164 collective nouns, beginning with those describing the 'beasts of the chase' but extending to include a wide range of animals and birds and an extensive array of human professions and types of person. *The Book of St Albans* was reprinted by the famous printer Wynkyn de Worde and new editions appeared throughout the sixteenth century, spreading the knowledge of these terms far beyond their early, elite audience.

Those collective nouns describing animals and birds have diverse sources of inspiration. Some are named for the characteristic behaviour of the animals (a leap of leopards, a busyness of ferrets), or by the use they were put to by humans (a yoke of oxen, a burden of mules). Sometimes they're given group nouns that describe their young (a covert of coots, a kindle of kittens), others by the way they respond when flushed (a sord of mallards, a rout of wolves). Others still are named by some personality trait they were believed to possess (a cowardice of curs, an unkindness of ravens). It's these examples that are most revealing of the medieval mind-set of their inventors, as well, of course, as those that describe people. Clearly there was no reason related to hunting that 'the companies of beasts and fowls' should have included terms, many of them humorous, sarcastic or negative in tone, to describe types of people or groups of craftsmen or professionals. The clergy come in for a particularly hard time, with 'an abominable sight of monks' and – gamely included by Dame Juliana – 'a superfluity of nuns'.

In exploring the origins of these, we owe much to earlier explorers of this terrain. James Lipton, whose book *An Exaltation of Larks* I have mentioned, not only looked back at the traditional terms but also ahead, challenging us all to join 'the game of venery' and invent our own set of terms for the modern age. Before him, in 1939, C. E. Hare's *The Language of Field Sports* gathers these terms neatly together with helpful notes on how they relate to the hunt. Earlier still, in 1909, John Eliot Hodgkin published a study titled *Proper Terms: An Attempt at a Rational Explanation of the Meanings of the Collection of Phrases in 'The Book of St Albans', 1486, Entitled 'The Compaynys of Beestys and Fowlys' and Similar Lists*. His approach was to try to prove that the majority of these terms were never originally intended as collective nouns at all, that they were meant simply to provide a guide to the correct words to use *in reference* to a particular animal or person, rather than as a group name. I don't subscribe to his theory but his insights and his meticulous poring through dictionaries of Middle English are invaluable in understanding the terms and the times they were written down in.

Most of the nouns that were used as hunting terms existed many years before they appeared in print in English and seem to have come from the French books of hunting that preceded them.

Thomas Malory's *Le Morte d'Arthur* points to the legendary Arthurian Knight Sir Tristram as their inventor, writing: 'And therefore the book of venery, of hawking, and hunting, is called the book of Sir Tristram. Wherefore, as meseemeth, all gentlemen that bear old arms ought of right to honour Sir Tristram for the goodly terms that gentlemen have and use, and shall to the day of doom, that thereby in a manner, all men of worship may dissever a gentleman from a yeoman, and from a yeoman, a villain.'

But the intentions of the creators of many of the nouns for animals that weren't hunted, and those for people, remain an enigma. Some are pure poetry, pithier and more poignant than a carefully crafted haiku. Others offer biting political satire, or a humorous glimpse of everyday life. Perhaps they were made up just for the joy of it; maybe they were designed as something to learn for the sake of being learned, like the poems that used to be recited by rote in schools. Or maybe it was intended that through regular use they would all eventually be accepted as 'proper' company terms. After all, a gaggle of geese appeared on these lists and none of us think twice about describing a flock of them as such. A pride of lions and a shoal of fish also appeared in print for the first time in these prescriptive medieval handbooks. Perhaps 500 years ago you'd have looked as foolish describing a flock of pheasants as a covey rather than a nye as you would today if you said you'd seen a pride of cows or a shoal of pigs.

We can't be sure why some terms have stood the test of time while others have fallen by the wayside; a few have made it into modern dictionaries but despite being deeply rooted in the history of the English language and indeed in the history of humanity, many are considered too fanciful and too little-used to warrant a place. They may not always be practical, they may often seem whimsical or idiosyncratic, but they share these traits with so many aspects of real life that to me they seem perfectly fit for purpose. They also allow us, from time to time, to follow the example of the nightingale and speak with the voice of our distant ancestors.

CHAPTER 1

PEOPLE

A FIGHTING OF BEGGARS

Modern users of this group name might be forgiven for assuming it has its roots in the rowdiness of medieval beggars, scrapping over a coin thrown by an uncharacteristically benevolent lord. But in his assessment of the phrase in his 1909 book *Proper Terms*, John Hodgkin tells us he thinks its listing as 'a fyting' in fifteenth-century texts offers a different source. The word *fyton* in Middle English meant mendacious or lying, which suggests the phrase came from the tendency of beggars to tell tall tales in the hope of obtaining alms.

Medieval England made no state provision for the destitute or homeless, who made up around twenty per cent of the country's population. The physically and mentally disabled, the blind, the deaf, the sick and the aged were left to fend for themselves with only the charity of the Church to support them. The truly needy often went without, while the canny fraudster made off with their share of the funds. Since the 1370s, London's law courts have dealt with cases of beggars who faked illness or infirmity in order to get the hand-outs afforded to those in real need. One court document records the case of two men who tried to gain charity by posing as merchants who had been robbed of everything and had their tongues cut out by their assailants. When it was revealed that in fact their tongues were perfectly intact and they had made the whole thing up, they were put in the stocks for three days. It's easy to see how 'a lying of beggars' might have taken root in the public consciousness.

A RASCAL OF BOYS

When this phrase for a group of boys was written down in fifteenth-century manuscripts, the word rascal was used in the same way that we use rabble or mob today. It referred not to an individual ruffian, but to a noisy, boisterous and trouble-making gang. It was also distinctly classist; sixteenth-century scholar Sir Thomas Smith describes Englishmen below the rank of Esquire as being divided into the subcategories of Gentlemen, Yeomen and Rascals in his 1560s book *De Republica Anglorum: the Maner of Gouernement or Policie of the Realme of England*. Rascals were at the bottom of the pile, hence the traditional children's rhyme: 'I'm the king of the castle, get down you dirty rascal.'

John Dryden's poetic political satire of 1681, *Absalom and Achitophel*, uses the word in this context:

> *Let Friendships holy*
> *Band some Names assure,*
> *Some their own Worth,*

and some let Scorn secure.
Nor shall the Rascal
Rabble here have Place,
Whom Kings no Titles gave,
and God no Grace.

Randall Cotgrave's *A French and English Dictionary* (1650) gives his definition of the word *peautraille* (meaning rabble) as, 'scrapings or offals of skins; and hence, a rascall, or base crue of scoundrells'. This image of rascals as the offal of society was reflected in the use of the term to describe vermin in the huntsman's vernacular. Young deer too small to be considered worth the effort of the hunt were also referred to as rascals.

Another, more sympathetic, collective noun appears in some of the lists for boys: 'a blush of boys', from the tendency of young boys to flush with colour when being caned, the usual punishment for being a little rascal.

AN INCREDULITY
OF CUCKOLDS

This must be the least likely of the collective nouns describing people to have been used in everyday medieval life. The idea of a group of husbands getting together to discuss their cheating wives seems unlikely even now, let alone in the fifteenth century. The fact that it appears in several of the early manuscripts shows how much of a game the invention of such terms had become by the mid 1400s, when the early highly formal hunting terms had given rise to an increasing number of wittier ones. What makes it especially fascinating to the modern mind is the light it sheds on male attitudes towards female sexuality and morality in the Middle Ages. This imaginary support group of husbands is incredulous to discover that their wives have been unfaithful to them. It's not a fury of cuckolds, or a weeping or a shamefulness, they're not in despair – they're either in denial or they're in the dark. The ideal wife was of course loyal and true, but sexual desire was acknowledged with more honesty in the Middle Ages than it has been in more recent times, especially when compared with the Victorian values that so often skew our sense of how things were perceived in the past. Several of Chaucer's *Canterbury Tales,* for example, dramatize adultery in a way that is more entertaining than judgemental. In 'The Miller's

Tale' the husband seems aware of the risks of taking a wife much younger than himself:

For she was wild and young,
and he was old,
And deemed himself as
like to be a cuckold.

The word cuckold is in fact linked to incredulity, in the sense of being unaware. It comes from the habit of the female cuckoo bird putting her eggs into other birds' nests, so a bird raising a chick that is not its own (or a man who finds himself raising another man's child) is called a cuckold.

A GAGGLE OF GOSSIPS

Gossip was rife in the Middle Ages for three reasons. First, privacy was hard to come by even in large homes since the grand hall was used by all family members and noble men and women were rarely out of the earshot of servants. There was also relatively little going on by way of passing the time compared to today. Finally, there were a lot more rules governing acceptable behaviour, so the kind of misdemeanours that would barely raise an eyebrow nowadays would have seemed scandalous to the medieval mind. This latter point meant that gossip could also be very damaging, and the besmirching of innocent reputations was such a problem that both borough and manorial courts tried to punish gossips with warnings and fines. Gossip was also a way of obtaining power in the Middle Ages, especially for women, to whom other means of exerting their influence were unavailable. Within court, rumours about who was in and who out of royal favour could subtly shift the balance of power, and in an age in which complete loyalty was paramount, rumours of allegiances elsewhere could be enough to see a nobleman stripped of his privileges.

A group of gossips has been described as a *gaggle* since the early fifteenth century at least, and the term appears in the Harley Manuscript and others. As with geese, the gaggle is an allusion to the sound made by those exchanging tittle-tattle.

James Lipton, in his 1993 book *An Exaltation of Larks*, offers 'a dish of gossips' and also 'a peek of gossip columnists' as a couple of modern variants.

◆ ◆ ◆

A HERD OF HARLOTS

The word harlot first appeared in print at the start of the thirteenth century and was then defined as a man of no fixed occupation, a vagabond or beggar. But a few years into the century it began to be used as a derogatory word for a certain kind of young woman. Prostitution was rife in medieval Britain and town records from the 1500s show that most towns and cities had at least one known brothel, some of which were publically owned. Thirteenth-century theologian St Thomas Aquinas wrote: 'If prostitution were to be suppressed, careless lusts would overthrow society.' But while they were an accepted part of life and often served the rich alongside the poor, prostitutes were regarded as part of the servile underclass. The Elizabethan sumptuary laws – intended to enforce social hierarchies by controlling how much money the people were allowed to spend on everything from food and wine to furniture and clothing – were strict when it came to the accepted apparel for prostitutes. They were expected to wear a coloured sash or striped hood to mark them out from respectable women and their right to ply their trade was restricted to certain streets or districts. Inevitably, though, as cities grew and spread, prostitutes would target those areas where they knew business would be best, congregating around public baths, popular taverns and universities. Calling a group of them 'a herd', as one might a group of livestock, was a way of labelling their lowliness.

A DAMNING OF JURORS

Appearing in *The Book of St Albans* as 'a dampnyng of jourrouris', this collective noun offers a window onto a pivotal part of British history. When King John signed the Magna Carta in 1215, he enshrined in law many of the precepts by which we still live today, including the right to a trial by jury. In his essay on the subject in 1852, pre-eminent American legal theorist Lysander Spooner translates the crucial clause as: 'No free man shall be captured or imprisoned or disseised of his freehold or of his liberties, or of his free customs, or be outlawed or exiled or in any way destroyed, nor will we proceed against him by force or proceed against him by arms, but by the lawful judgment of his peers or by the law of the land.'

Before the thirteenth century the old feudal system of justice prevailed, under which anyone accused of a crime could be charged, tried and sentenced by the lord of the manor and his staff. Later justices were appointed to attend courts of assizes, quarterly court sessions where visiting judges were responsible for sentencing. Even with the advent of trial by jury, the judge still had a large role to play in determining the outcome of a trial and the jury would take their lead from him. A 'damning' verdict was one that found the plaintiff guilty of the crimes they were charged with. The word comes from the Old French word *dampner*, from the Latin *damnāre*, meaning to injure or condemn, and in the God-fearing Middle Ages, it implied that your crimes made you worthy of eternal damnation.

A BEVY OF LADIES

This term dates back to the earliest manuscripts and John Kersey's *New English Dictionary* of 1702 describes it as 'the proper term for a company of maidens or ladies, of roes, of quails or of larks'. This would have been reserved for women in the upper tiers of society – note that they share the noun with delicate creatures like deer and birds – in contrast to women of ill-repute, who were grouped in with cattle (see 'a herd of harlots'). However, roes, quails and larks were still quarry, owned by the lord of the manor, so in a way it seems a fitting noun from a modern perspective, since 'ladies' were as much the property of their noble husbands as the livestock. By law, ownership of a young noblewoman passed from her father to her husband when she married, though in certain circumstances ladies did wield more power in the Middle Ages than they were allowed in subsequent centuries, handling the finances and the running of the manor whenever their husbands were away. Their main role, though, was to produce an heir, so ladies spent most of their lives pregnant. Some 20 per cent of women died in childbirth, making the average life expectancy of even the most high born of women just forty years. No one really knows where the word bevy came from, or why it is used to describe ladies, though Hodgkin does suggest that since roes can most often be seen in groups while at the watering hole, the term may first have been applied to them.

A RAGE OF MAIDENS

Listed as a rage or rag in the fifteenth-century lists, this term comes from the medieval word rage, which meant romp, or play wantonly. Chaucer's 'The Miller's Tale' provides a fine example of the word in context: 'Now Sir, and eft Sir, so befell the cas / That on a day this heende Nicholas / Fit with this yonge wyf to rage and pleye / Whil that hir housbond was at Oseney.' (In translation: Now sir, and again sir, it so chanced that this gentle Nicholas fell to romp and play with this young wife, while her husband was at Osney.) Whether the originators of this phrase had the urges of the maidens or those who wished to romp with them in mind when they conceived it is impossible to judge, but as Chaucer's young Miller's wife shows, women's desires were acknowledged far more freely in the fifteenth century than they would be a century or two later. Arthurian Romance literature was popular with young women, including those from noble families, by the late middle age, and exploration of the books left by women in their wills reveals that the most popular of these were the stories about Lancelot and Tristan, which featured passionate adultery on the part of their heroines. In the Middle Ages, maidenhood began at around the age of twelve. There was no ceremonial rite of passage but it was regarded as a period of transformation from girlhood to womanhood, and was considered to represent a kind of perfect age. James Lipton's modern variants, 'a slouch of models' and 'a rictus of beauty queens', offer a different perception of youthful beauty.

A SKULK OF THIEVES

Times were tough in the 1400s. Successive hard winters meant that crops often failed and harvests didn't produce enough food to sustain the population, while the move towards livestock farming meant that many agricultural workers found themselves without the means to make a living. Between 20 and 30 per cent of the population of medieval Europe were considered destitute and many died of starvation or disease caused by poverty. It's easy to see how such conditions led desperate people to steal, and thirteenth- and fourteenth-century coroners' inquests provide a written record of some of the tragic ends they met, often in the act of trying to provide for their hungry families. One inquest tells the sad story of a thief falling from a ladder to his death while trying to steal a ham hanging from a beam in the roof of a peasant's house.

In the towns and cities pickpocketing was also rife and in some areas gangs of thieves would work together to rob the wealthy as they travelled through the countryside. Their prowling behaviour, hanging back in the shadows until they saw a likely target, fits well with the collective noun devised for them, which they share with foxes and friars. The penalties for theft were initially fines, but as the offences became more serious, and the amounts stolen increased, the punishment worsened. Some thieves were flogged; others had an ear or a hand cut off. The most serious offenders were hanged. But for many petty criminals, it was a risk worth taking.

CHAPTER 2

PROFESSIONS

A TABERNACLE OF BAKERS

Bread was the mainstay of a medieval peasant's diet, with meat, fish and dairy produce too expensive to be eaten any more than once or twice a week and only then in small quantities. While the rich dined on venison, partridge and quail, the poor ate soups made from root vegetables and whatever grain they could lay their hands on. This dependency on bread as a staple food meant that strict laws were put in place to govern its distribution. These were enforced even more fiercely after the Great Famine of 1315-1317, when repeated crop failures meant that grain harvests produced far less food than was needed to feed the starving populations of Europe.

The law stated that no baker was allowed to sell his bread from beside his own oven and must instead purvey his produce at one of the King's approved markets. Any baker found selling his bread from his own home or a private shop was fined, so most set up stalls at markets. These small, portable shops were known in Middle English as 'tabernacula', which is defined in Dutch lexicographer Junius Hadrianus' *The Nomenclator* – a book written in 1585 'containing proper names and apt terms for all things under their convenient titles' – as 'little shops made of boards'. The word came to English via Old French from the Latin word *tabernāculum*, meaning tent or hut, though there may have been some crossover with the tabernacle described in the Hebrew Bible as a sort of mobile home for the divine presence during the exodus from Egypt.

A GORING OF BUTCHERS

There was good reason for the invention of a collective noun for butchers in fifteenth-century England. Since as early as 975, butchers had organized themselves in order to encourage good practice and trade and by 1272 they had formed the Butchers' Guild. In 1331 this guild was afforded the right to regulate the trade, establishing rules for the slaughter of livestock and the merchandising of meat. The group name is apt because in the Middle Ages all the produce butchers sold came from animals they had slaughtered themselves. Before refrigeration was possible, fresh meat would only stay that way for a few days and there was no safe way of transporting meat once the animal was dead. Dedicated slaughterhouses, now called abattoirs, weren't established until the eighteenth century.

Medieval butchers might therefore slaughter several animals at the start of each week and keep them until they'd sold out or the meat went bad. A trip to the butcher's shop was not for the faint-hearted and the inspiration for 'a goring' of butchers could well have been their blood-spattered, gore-covered aprons. The word 'gore' comes from the Old English *gor*, meaning dirt or filth. 'A goring' could also have its roots in the verb 'to gore', meaning to pierce or stab as a bull might with his horns, or, perhaps, as a butcher might with his freshly sharpened knife.

A DRAUGHT OF BUTLERS

Found in many early collections, this is another group noun for people with a markedly satirical tone. Butlers get their name from the fact that in the wealthy houses in which they served, their primary duty was to take charge of the buttery, where the butts of wine were stored. The word butler comes from the late twelfth-century Anglo-French word *butellier*, meaning cup-bearer. And a 'butt' was the name given to the half-toun barrel the wine was stored in. Incidentally, King Edward IV's rebellious brother George, the Duke of Clarence, was rumoured to have been deliberately drowned in a butt of wine while he awaited execution in the Tower of London (legend has it that he was offered the chance to choose the method by which he would die and he selected submersion in a rather fine Malmsey).

A lot of wine was drunk in the noble households of the Middle Ages and the need for careful storage and regular tasting meant that taking care of the wine was a full-time job. It was the butler's responsibility to select the wines his master might most enjoy and to do this properly he usually sampled the wine to check its suitability for the fine palates of those above stairs. The 'draught' referred to the tasting sample of wine drawn off for him to taste, and this collective noun seems to be mischievously suggesting that the draught might be the butler's favourite part of his job.

A DRUNKSHIP OF COBBLERS

Drunkship, meaning a group of drunken people, has fallen into disuse in modern times but is surely ripe for a resurgence. Lexicologist John Kersey's *A New English Dictionary*, published in 1702, was the first dictionary of the English language to include words in common usage, in addition to the 'difficult' words that previous dictionaries had made their focus. He defines drunkship as 'a drunken company'.

Cobblers in medieval England were at the lower end of the tradesman's pecking order; their job was simply to repair shoes, making them the poorer cousin of the shoemaker, or cordwainer, who designed and made the shoes. The reason for cobblers to have been singled out from amongst the other lowlier trades as being particularly prone to drunkenness is lost to the annals of time, but it's safe to assume that they were representative of the working tradesman of the day and therefore probably enjoyed a drink or two once their week's work was done.

In fact, though, like most medieval members of the lower classes, cobblers would have drunk ale on a daily basis as part of their normal fluid intake. Water couldn't be trusted as a means of hydration because of the difficulties of keeping it clean. In towns and cities the water supply doubled as a sewerage system and diseases like typhoid were widespread and justly

feared. Instead, the rich drank wine and the poor drank ale. These were watered down for daily use, and were consumed by everyone, with every meal. Children were given ale after they turned five. For the under-fives milk was favoured and ale was avoided, but only because it might have curdled the milk.

A HASTINESS OF COOKS

This appeared in Lydgate's 'Horse, Sheep and Goose' and in *The Book of St Albans*, but while its origins are ancient, the inspiration behind it is open to interpretation.

Large-scale cooking in the Middle Ages was a tricky business. The food would be prepared on rough wooden trestle tables in the vast caverns of the kitchen while the main fire was readied for the spit, where huge cuts of meat and often whole pigs were roasted over the open flames. Other foods were boiled together in a large cauldron, wrapped in pieces of cloth to keep them separate. Before a big castle feast there would be many cooks (certainly enough to spoil the broth) hurriedly working to get everything ready to serve, so 'a hastiness' could well have been an accurate description. In the learned opinion of John Hodgkin though, the term is meant ironically, medieval cooks being in fact the opposite of hasty, especially when a hungry nobleman was impatient for his feast.

Another group name for cooks that appears in some modern collections is 'a mystery'. While this does pleasingly reflect the talented chef's ability to conjure up delicious concoctions, its source is rather more prosaic. When charters were handed out to the trades in the fifteenth century the resulting guild was known as a mystery. The preamble to King Edward IV's charter read: '. . . the freemen of the Mystery of Cooks have for a long time personally taken and borne, and to this day do not cease to take and bear, great and manifold pains and labour as well at our great feast of St. George and at others according to our command.'

A SQUAT OF DAUBERS

Daubers were the plasterers-cum-bricklayers of the Middle Ages, responsible for the application of daub – a sticky mixture of clay, sand, damp earth, animal dung and straw – to wattle, which was a wooden lattice that made the structure of walls in medieval houses. The statute of labourers in the late fourteenth century created records of litigation relating to house building that make reference to the many trades involved. Carpenters were the primary workers but specialist thatchers, masons and daubers all get a mention.

It's easy enough to imagine the dauber squatting down beside his handiwork, hunched over the woven woodwork of the wattle to spread on the daub, but in fact our modern sense of the word squat, meaning crouch, has only been used since the seventeenth century. This collective noun appears on the fifteenth-century manuscripts and must therefore have its origins in an earlier meaning of the word, given by the *Oxford English Dictionary* (*OED*) as 'thrust down with force', which comes from the Old French *esquatir*, meaning 'flatten'. This forceful downward motion by which the daub was applied worked to press the granular mixture into any fissures in the woven wood – usually split saplings of hazel and ash – making the resulting structure secure and as resistant to the wind and rain as could be hoped for.

In his *An Exaltation of Larks*, James Lipton takes inspiration from these nouns describing house-building trades and offers 'a clamber of roofers', 'a panel of carpenters' and 'a drip of roof painters'.

◆ ◆ ◆

A DRIFT OF FISHERMEN

Not much is known about fishing before the seventeenth century. Most fishermen were illiterate and kept no records of their methods. Once again Dame Juliana Barnes comes to our aid with her *Treatise of Fysshynge with an Angle,* the earliest printed document about fishing. She details a range of different flies that could be used, though it seems likely given the context of the treatise – it appears alongside her works on hunting and hawking in Wynkyn de Worde's version – that the fishing she describes is angling for sport, rather than fishing for a living.

As a profession, fishing was all-important in the Middle Ages. Fish stocks were plentiful and unlike farm animals, fish required no outlay to feed or shelter them before they could be killed and eaten, which made them a good value food. Fish was also in demand because it was allowed on days of abstinence – the days of the week that the Church decreed should be passed without eating meat. These totalled almost half the year: every Friday and Saturday and the whole of Lent and Advent Wednesdays too. As a result, fish and seafood were as important as meat in the diets of the upper classes.

The range of fish eaten included herring, salmon, eel, whiting, plaice, cod, trout and pike, as well as shellfish such as crab, oysters, mussels and cockles. Because of the difficulty of keeping food fresh without refrigeration, large quantities of salted and smoked fish were consumed. But it wasn't until the mid-1600s that fishing boats worked in pairs, dragging a net between them. Until then boats stayed in coastal waters, drifting with the tide until they'd caught their fill.

A MELODY OF HARPERS

Depicted in wall paintings of Ancient Egyptian tombs, the harp is one of the oldest musical instruments in the world. Originally made in the shape of a hunter's bow, by the Middle Ages they closely resembled the Gaelic harp as we know it today and were experiencing a surge in popularity in the age of troubadours and minstrels. As the lists of venereal terms we're exploring in this book reveal, this was an era defined by its emphasis on knightly tradition. Just as a nobleman had to know the proper way of referring to animals of the hunt, his conduct had to honour the knights who had so bravely returned from the crusades, and his behaviour in court had to reflect his understanding of the codes of chivalry. This was good news for harpists. Their melodious music was seen as the perfect expression of purity and the harp often accompanied songs about valiant deeds and courtly love. In great demand at the estates of the upper classes, travelling harpists and other musicians of gentle instruments like lutes, viols and flutes, often moved from town to town performing instrumental accompaniment at banquets and recitals of madrigal singing.

There were high-born harpists, too. The instrument was deemed elegant enough to be taught to the children of the nobility and both Henry VIII and Anne Boleyn were keen players. In fact the harp had been established in the royal household since

Henry IV, whose reign ended in 1413, which perhaps explains why this group name for harpists is so flattering.

In his book *An Exaltation of Larks*, James Lipton adds to the range of terms describing musicians with 'a meter of percussionists', 'a flatulence of bassoonists' and 'a backache of double-bassists'.

A LAUGHTER OF HOSTELERS

Of all the collective nouns describing people in the medieval lists, this is one of the most affectionate, which can perhaps be explained by the fact that the hosteler was the provider of comfortable lodgings, food and strong ale. Appearing as 'a laughtre of osteloris' in *The Book of St Albans*, the term evokes an image of the jolly, welcoming and possibly not 100 per cent sober proprietor of a fourteenth-century inn. In the early part of the century such establishments were rare; the reason for most long journeys was pilgrimage, and wealthy abbeys and monasteries had traditionally provided shelter and nourishment for such travellers in return for a small donation, and sometimes out of charity if the visitor was too poor to pay. But after Henry VIII's dissolution of the monasteries in the 1530s, many taverns turned themselves into inns where the weary traveller could get a bed and a stable for his horse along with his quart of ale.

Perhaps the most famous example of such an establishment was the Tabard near London Bridge in Southwark, the starting point for Chaucer's *Canterbury Tales*, while the most famous hosteler must be the pilgrims' host, Harry Bailey, a good-humoured fellow who suggests the telling of tales as a form of entertainment on the journey to Canterbury. Chaucer's description of him suggests he was the archetypal laughing hosteler:

. . . he was a very merry man,
And after meat, at playing he began,
Speaking of mirth among some other things,
When all of us had paid our reckonings.

A SENTENCE OF JUDGES

Up until the twelfth century, there were no such things as judges. The law was deeply rooted in the feudal system, whereby the lord of the manor could charge and punish perpetrators of crime – often poaching from his land – as he saw fit. Most punishments involved the paying of a fine, the proceeds of which of course went straight into the lord of the manor's coffers. But in 1166, Henry II sought to shift the power away from individual landowners and bring it more directly under his own control. He issued a declaration which established a new system – the courts of assizes, where a national bench of judges travelled around the country attending quarterly court sessions at which they heard the more serious cases in each town.

Not all kinds of crimes were tried at each assizes, which meant that many people accused of crime spent months waiting in prison for an official sentence to be passed, but importantly, instead of applying local law, these judges based their decisions on a new set of national laws which were common to all people. This is where we get the term 'common law'. Which cases the judges would hear were decided on by a jury of local men, since there was no police force to charge people, and petty crimes were dealt with by justices of the peace in magistrates' courts. Though more egalitarian than the manorial system, assizes judges could be harsh in the sentences they delivered, which ranged from a stint in the stocks to public execution.

AN ELOQUENCE OF LAWYERS

When this noun appeared in *The Book of St Albans* in 1486, the justice system was just beginning to emerge from the grip of feudalism (see 'a sentence of judges'). Lords had professional pleaders working for them who represented the interests of the manorial estate in the county courts and pleaders could also be used to represent the plaintiff. These were laymen rather than ordained clerics, who had previously been the only ones with training in law, and as they became experienced and sought after, they began to charge a fee for their work and the legal profession was born.

By the fourteenth century the four Inns of Court – the Inner and Middle Temple, Lincoln's Inn and Gray's Inn – had been founded in London to provide formalized training for lawyers. By the end of the fifteenth century pleaders had come to be called barristers and a structured system of education in the law was in place. Students would spend seven years at the Inns of Court, studying, attending lectures and watching established pleaders at work, absorbing both the ethos of their profession and the discursive arguing style it is known for to this day. With the success of their career depending entirely on their ability to convince a judge of their point, eloquence was the most important attribute a lawyer could have.

James Lipton's *An Exaltation of Larks* suggests 'an escheat of lawyers' and also delves into the modern legal system with 'a presumption of prosecutors'.

A FAITH OF MERCHANTS

Faith as it is used here was a reference to the trustworthiness of a person, rather than in the religious sense of the word, and is meant ironically, since merchants were rarely trusted. The noun appeared in *The Book of St Albans* and provides a window onto the world of medieval trading. Merchants lived outside the rigid structure of feudalism and their growing success in the fifteenth century had an enormous impact on the shape and structure of society.

Resentful of the huge taxes levied on their profits, merchants joined forces and formed guilds of fellow traders. With strength in numbers, they were able to negotiate better terms from the lords who owned the land they worked from. Eventually, these guilds began to buy charters directly from the King, which allowed the towns to become independent of the lord of the manor. Many merchants took up the positions of authority in these newly chartered towns and set new rules dictating who could trade there. The guilds also provided protection for their members, which effectively meant setting prices so they couldn't be undercut. This gave those outside the guilds the impression that they were not to be trusted, since they were always out to protect their interests and maximize their own profits.

Court documents from the time record the various tricks of the trade that were sometimes used to con the public, including hiding bad grain under good, stitching undersized coal sacks to disguise small measures of coal, selling fresh produce on the edge of going bad and plain old overpricing. All of these were officially punishable by a stint in the pillory, but because the guilds were self-regulated, most perpetrators got off with only a fine, to the inevitable anger of the masses.

A modern-day addition to this phrase can be found in James Lipton's *An Exaltation of Larks*, where he suggests 'an ambush of used-car dealers'.

A MISBELIEF OF PAINTERS

We're talking artists here, rather than decorators, and, in particular, painters of portraits. The aim of medieval portraiture was to present the sitter as they hoped to be remembered after their death. The aspects of a subject that were held to be most significant to posterity in the Middle Ages were

not the precise shade of pink in a cheek or the exact thickness of an eyebrow, but the symbols that represented social status. In fact, observational portraiture, painted from a live subject, only became common towards the end of the Middle Ages. And once artists did have a real person in front of them, it became even more important that the person was flattered by the portrait. Artists, like poets, were dependent on wealthy patrons for their living so portrait painters had to strike a balance between truthfulness and flattery. Shoulders could be broadened, eyes brightened, paunches flattened and foreheads heightened. As long as the clothing and heraldry were accurate, the rest could be tweaked as much as necessary to coax the sitter into commissioning the artist again and paying a handsome fee.

The Book of St Albans lists 'a misbeleue of paynters', which, not to be confused with disbelieve, meant an erroneous belief, rather than an inability or refusal to believe. The painter's job was to conjure misbelief in those who viewed his work, to create the illusion of beauty even where he found none.

AN IMPERTINENCE
OF PEDDLERS

Selling goods from door to door was a fairly new thing in medieval times. The feudal system had traditionally kept everyone tied to the land, with the poorest forced to work for the lord of the manor, even when wages were low and poor harvests left them hungry. But as farms began to switch from agriculture to livestock and many labourers found themselves without work, some made ends meet by procuring and selling on household items like fabrics, needles, ribbons and cutlery, which they hawked on the street or took from home to home. In rural areas where more unusual items were harder to find at the local markets, pedlars added wine, rosary beads, lace, eyeglasses and spices to their haul of wares. They were heavily taxed and often struggled to make a profit, so usually charged as high a price as they thought they could get away with, which gave them a reputation for dishonesty.

In 1566 early sociologist Thomas Harman published a book detailing the lives of those living on the fringes of English society titled *A Caveat or Warning for Common Cursetors, Vulgarly Called Vagabonds* in which he sums up the popular Elizabethan view of peddlers 'as much as they seek gain unlawfully against the laws and statues of this noble realm, they are well worthy to be registered among the number of vagabonds.' The impertinence of those pushing their goods was also referenced in a medieval proverb well known in the fifteenth century: 'A peddler always praises his wares.'

Lipton brings this one up to date with 'a push of peddlers' and also offers 'a persistence of insurance salesmen'.

A SUBTLETY OF SERGEANTS

At first glance this seems an incongruous pairing of words. In the UK the rank of police sergeant, one up from the entry-level constable, requires bravery, discipline and attention to detail, but not subtlety. Of course, this term features in *The Book of St Albans*, which pre-dates the existence of a police force by 400 years, so we must turn to the Harley Manuscripts, which include a collection of works by fifteenth-century cleric and poet John Lydgate, for an explanation. In 'Measure is Treasure' from his *Minor Poems*, Lydgate writes of:

> *Trew juges and sergeantis of the lawe,*
> *For hate or frenshippe they shal ther doomys dresse.*

In the 1400s a sergeant of the law was the name given to senior lawyers. In the newly emerging legal profession there were two distinct groups of lawyer: attorneys, who dealt with procedural and administrative matters, and serjeants, who were also known as 'pleaders' and whose role was to speak on behalf of the plaintiff. Convincing a judge of the infallibility of their case required both a steely grasp of the statute book and the ability to construct a finely tuned argument. Subtlety was everything.

Whether the medieval interpretation of this was straightforward or satirical is hard to judge. It could be among the many seemingly tongue-in-cheek group names devised for the professions (see 'an obedience of servants' and 'a discretion of priests' among others) and in keeping with this interpretation James Lipton adds to the collection with some terms for modern-day military version: 'a glower of sergeants', 'a bellow of drill sergeants' and 'an indigestion of mess sergeants'.

AN OBEDIENCE OF SERVANTS

Appearing in the Egerton Manuscript as an 'obedyens of seruandys', John Hodgkin suggests that this term is one of the many that are sarcastic in tone. There is certainly a playfulness about many of the collective nouns that refer to trades and professions and since the lists were originally intended as part of an education in the ways of the nobleman, this could well have been a little knowing nod to the difficulties of overseeing a house served by wayward staff.

There were certainly plenty of staff members to keep in line; an average upper-class family in medieval England kept between 100 and 200 servants. Every task necessary for the running of the home and the care of the noble family had an individual servant assigned to it, from tasting the wine (see 'a draught of butlers') to emptying the chamber pots. This created a hierarchy among servants that mirrored the structure of society at large. Obedience to senior members of staff and to the family was expected at all times and any servant breaking the rules of the house faced harsh penalties, most often in the form of a fine or a cut in wages. Where troublemaking became more serious a servant might be flogged, or if they attempted to escape their masters, they could even be tried. Legislation passed in 1414 included an act giving justices the power to issue writs to the sheriffs for fugitive labourers, including servants, who had fled from one county to another. High-born families lived with large numbers of servants and presumably hoped they'd be 'an obedience'.

A DISGUISING OF TAILORS

What people wore really mattered in the Middle Ages. Clothes weren't just an expression of your taste or personality; they were a reflection of your position in society. By the time Elizabeth I took to the throne the extravagant fashions of the age were taking their toll on the pockets of the nobility. Debt and even bankruptcy were rife among high-born families and the new Queen was determined to put a stop to this scandal in her court. She was also keen to underscore the boundaries between the tiers in the social pecking order that had been blending and slipping with the rise of the wealthy but low-born merchant classes.

Her solution was to introduce sumptuary laws, which dictated the goods and clothes that could be purchased by each class of person and which were strictly prescriptive about the fabrics, colours and cuts that were permitted. In a climate in which the preservation of strict traditional hierarchies was paramount, anyone seen to be dressing in a manner unsuited to their station was regarded with suspicion. Shakespeare uses clothing as a means of disguising his characters in many of his plays – most dramatically, to allow women to be mistaken for men. In *As You Like It*, Rosalind, a duke's daughter, is transformed into a shepherd; in *The Merchant of Venice* Portia becomes a male lawyer; in *Twelfth Night*, Viola becomes a pageboy. The clothes of a gentleman conferred the status of a gentleman, and in this way, the tailor was uniquely equipped to provide a disguise.

A PROMISE OF TAPSTERS

Though it shares the same fifteenth-century origins as the other terms of assembly explored in this book, with a little linguistic updating this one could have been made for the modern world. 'Tapster' is now obsolete but can be translated as barman or barmaid – whoever is in charge of the 'tap' at the tavern of your choice.

The tapster's 'promise' is something we're all familiar with: that slight inclination of the chin, subtle nod or lift of the eyebrow that says, 'Yes, you may be embedded in the boozy armpit of the person next to you having jostled for half an hour to make it to the bar but relax, I have registered your place in the queue and you're up next.' There's never been a better embodiment of a false promise than the tapster's. It can't be trusted now and it couldn't be trusted then. In Shakespeare's *As You Like It,* Celia and Rosalind make the point perfectly in their discussion about the promises of love with the damning line: 'The oath of a lover is no stronger than the word of a tapster.'

A GLOZING OF
TAVERNERS

Glozing is a Middle English word meaning fawning, so we might modernise this noun, which appeared in this form in *The Book of St Albans,* to read 'a fawning of pub landlords'. For a more precise sense of the way in which the word might have been used we can refer to its origins in the Old French word *gloser*, from *glose*, which the OED says means 'a gloss, comment'. It was a kind of gilding of the truth, flattery in its truest sense, as in making more of something than it deserves, and in this sense it wasn't wholly honest. In fact, it was a means to an end.

Taverns were everywhere in the late Middle Ages, from substantial city breweries to tiny living rooms offering the latest home brew. Along with spinning and animal husbandry, brewing was a common way for medieval peasants to supplement their family income, and with so many people turning their hands to ale-making, competition was fierce. 'A glozing of taverners' is a reference to the necessity for taverners to flatter their patrons, making them feel welcome and appreciated if they wanted to keep their custom and prevent them from taking their beer money to line the pockets of the rival taverner next door. Most established taverns had other ways of enticing back customers, including the supply of cards and dice for games, or in certain establishments, the provision of prostitutes – a group of whom might also well be described as a glozing, if they weren't already down as a herd (see 'a herd of harlots').

◆ ◆ ◆

A WANDERING OF TINKERS

To the order- and hierarchy-obsessed upper echelons of medieval society, the wandering tinker represented everything that they most feared about a post-feudal world. A by-product of the switch from arable to livestock farming, most tinkers had found themselves without work to do on the land, and rather than trying to find work for another lord of the manor, they had set up on their own to make what money they could by doing odd jobs, repair work and occasional labour door to door. They were the archetypal 'masterless men' that featured so prominently in religious and philosophical warnings about societal breakdown in the medieval era and they had a reputation for idleness and poor discipline.

In 1566 sociologist Thomas Harman included the tinker in his book *A Caveat or Warning for Common Cursetors, Vulgarly Called Vagabonds*:

> *I was credibly informed by such as could well tell, that one of these tippling Tinkers with his dog robbed by the highway four Pallyards six persons together, and took from them about four pounds in ready money, and hid him after in a thick wood a day or two and so escaped untaken. Thus with picking and stealing, mingled with a little work for a colour, they pass their time.*

Such was their place in popular culture that the profession appeared in a rhyme used by young girls in a counting game that playfully suggested how their future would unfold. 'What will my husband be?' the girl would ask, before counting her buttons or beans to find the answer as she chanted: 'Tinker, tailor, soldier, sailor, rich-man, poor-man, beggarman, thief.'

A WORSHIP OF WRITERS

This at first ambiguous collective noun in fact reveals a great deal about the way that writers lived in the Middle Ages. Britain's first printing press was established by William Caxton in 1476 and before this the only books in circulation were handwritten. Even once the press was up and running, each letter had to be individually set, there were no big printing runs, and there was certainly no money to be made from book sales. The only way that writers could earn a living by their pens was to attract the support of a wealthy patron. And patrons weren't the altruistic supporters of the arts that we're familiar with today. They expected something in return for their money, and at the very least they expected kind things to be said about them by the writer they'd chosen to help. Eighteenth-century literary historian Thomas

Wharton describes the system in his *History of English Poetry* as 'the established tyranny of patronage'. He is critical of a system that compels writers to include fawning dedications with every new piece of work. Both Chaucer – who spent much of his time at court – and the English poet of courtly love John Gower were bound in this way to Henry IV himself. On receipt of a grant for wine from the King, Gower wrote in his poem 'In Praise of Peace':

> *As y which evere unto my lives ende*
> *Wol praie for the stat of thi persone*
> *In worschipe of thi sceptre and of thi throne.*

CHAPTER 3

RELIGIOUS CALLINGS

A SKULK OF FRIARS

Friars were roaming priests who had no ties to a monastery, but who could nonetheless administer the sacraments, including baptism, matrimony, Holy Communion, the hearing of confession and granting of penance. The word friar simply means brother. Friars belonged to a holy order, to which they took vows of poverty and committed to living only on what they could beg for. But Catholic guilt was so pervasive at the time that friars often made comfortable livings from the donations of people anxious to be absolved of their sins. Their autonomy made them suspicious in the eyes of the establishment, and their reputation for profiteering meant they were also distrusted by the people.

Popular attitudes towards friars are revealed in Chaucer's characterization of Hubert the Friar in his *Canterbury Tales*. He describes him as a lecherous rogue, spending more time with women than with the sick or needy.

> *In towns he knew the taverns, every one,*
> *And every good host and each barmaid too –*
> *Better than begging lepers, these he knew.*

Later Chaucer implies friars are money-grabbing, exchanging forgiveness for cash:

Instead of weeping and of prayer,
Men ought to give some silver to
the poor frères

They share a group name with foxes and thieves, and, as Chaucer suggests, many were simply tricksters using the cloak of religion to con people into giving them money. The fact that they were not attached to a monastery or church probably added to the appropriateness of the word 'skulk' since they had to loiter in places where they could most readily take advantage of the guilty consciences in need of absolution.

AN OBSERVANCE OF HERMITS

The *New English Dictionary*, published in 1702, defined this term as 'a company of religious persons observing some rule, or belonging to some order'. And though a company of hermits seems like something of an oxymoron, since hermits are by definition solitary, many of those who chose a life of religious devotion lived in like-minded communities, either in monasteries or convents or in more widely spread-out hermitages, gathering occasionally for prayer. While we now use the word hermit to describe anyone who has withdrawn from society and become a recluse, in medieval times it applied specifically to those whose choice came from religious conviction. It was based on the theology of the Old Testament, which advocated seclusion and hardship – modelled on Jesus's forty days in the desert – as the key to spiritual development.

Several new religious orders were formed in the High Middle Ages: the Cistercians, Carthusians and Camaldolese all allowed their members to live as hermits and had strict codes that had to be carefully observed. But not all hermits were attached to a specific order. Many led their own lives of devotion living in huts or cells on the edges of towns and villages, sometimes earning enough to live on by doing odd jobs or begging for the funds to complete socially useful tasks such as building bridges or repairing lighthouses.

AN ABOMINABLE SIGHT OF MONKS

Of all the nouns describing people or professions this is surely the most comical. But John Hodgkin tells us this one, along with 'a superfluity of nuns', is 'no sarcastic allusion, but the plain belief bluntly stated'.

Monks weren't particularly popular with the masses (no pun intended) during the fifteenth century. In fact, they'd been widely hated by the populace since the arrival of the Christian Church. In Bede's *Life of Cuthbert*, dated around AD 725, is the story of a party of monks who almost drowned when their boat was caught in a storm on the River Tyne. Cuthbert pleaded with the peasants on the bank for help but 'the rustics, turning on him with angry minds and angry mouths, exclaimed, "Nobody shall pray for them: may God spare none of them! For they have taken away from men the ancient rites and customs, and how the new ones are to be attended to, nobody knows."'

By the fifteenth century this resentment of the trampling of pagan traditions had been exacerbated by a perception of monks as greedy and over-privileged.

While the general population starved, the monks were well fed and comfortable.

Abominable is defined by the *OED* as 'causing moral revulsion', which is a fairly accurate description of the reaction this image provoked. The Middle English word comes from the Latin *abominabilis*, and was once widely believed to stem from *ab*, meaning 'away from' and *homine* from *homo*, meaning 'human being'. Right up to the seventeenth century it was often spelt 'abhominable'.

A SUPERFLUITY OF NUNS

The Harley Manuscript has the far more respectful 'a reverent holynesse of nunys', which, though accurate, is far less illuminating. From all the other medieval lists comes 'superfluyte', which can be interpreted in one of two ways. The first is as simple fact; there were around 138 nunneries in England between 1270 and 1536, many of which were severely overcrowded. In her 1922 book *Medieval Nunneries*, Cambridge academic Eileen Power explains that during these years, convents were 'aristocratic institutions, the refuge of the gently born'. The convent was seen as a natural step for the daughters of the nobility who had passed marriageable age.

Power quotes from the will of one Sir John le Blund, who in 1312 bequeathed an annuity to his daughter Anne 'till she marry or enter a religious house', and explains that lords put pressure on prioresses to accept their daughters even if they were already full. This helps to put Juliana Barnes, the apparent author of *The Book of St Albans*, into context. Brought up at court and living among other high-born women as the prioress of a convent at Sopwell, it makes sense that she'd have been so familiar with the rules of hunting, and that she'd have known about the superfluity of nuns.

Alternatively though, the excess of nuns recorded in *The Book of St Albans* could have been a reference to the emerging view among agitators for Church reform that the days of the monastery and convent were over. Fifty years after *The Book of St Albans* was printed, Henry VIII ordered their closure and the Protestant Reformation was in full swing.

James Lipton's modern version is 'a flap of nuns', whom he accompanies with 'a fidget of altar boys' and 'a calendar of saints'.

A LYING OF PARDONERS

Medieval society was dominated by the Church and the Church taught that the ticket into heaven was an unsullied soul. In pursuit of spiritual purity but largely unable to resist the temptation to commit the occasional wrongdoing, the desperate populace turned to 'pardoners' to cleanse them of their sins.

Pardoners were usually friars or priests who claimed to be in close contact with the Pope, whom they said gave them the power to grant absolution. For a fee, naturally. Since quality controlling the cleansing of a soul was rather tricky, this profession seemed to attract a large number of fraudsters armed with fake papal pardons and bogus relics.

For modern-day cynics the whole concept of this is clearly a con, but even ardent medieval believers felt hard done by when they discovered that the pardoner they'd put their trust in had never even been to Rome. Records held by the Corporation of the City of London dating back to the fifteenth century reveal several cases of 'lying pardoners' being put in the stocks for this offence and Chaucer's Pardoner, as these lines from *The Canterbury Tales* illustrate, is typical of his kind:

His wallet lay before
him in his lap,
Stuffed full of pardons brought
from Rome all hot [...]
For in his bag he
had a pillowcase
The which, he said, was
Our True Lady's veil:
He said he had a piece
of the very sail
That good Saint Peter had,
what time he went
Upon the sea, till Jesus
changed his bent.
He had a latten cross
set full of stones,
And in a bottle had he
some pig's bones.
But with these relics,
when he came upon
Some simple parson,
then this paragon
In that one day more
money stood to gain
Than the poor dupe in
two months could attain.

A CONVERTING OF PREACHERS

The manuscripts in which these traditional collective nouns appeared were being written on the cusp of the Protestant Reformation. English scholar and lay preacher John Wycliffe had attracted a strong following of supporters – known as the Lollards – with his anticlerical ideas for reform in fourteenth century, and *The Book of St Albans* was completed three years after the birth of Martin Luther, whose arguments would become the lynchpin of the movement.

Preachers carrying this message of dissent often spoke in public places out in the open, following the example of Jesus' Sermon on the Mount, in the hope of getting their beliefs heard by as many people as possible. They often found large open spaces on the edges of towns to avoid being noticed by the authorities, whose loyalties at that time still lay firmly with the Catholic Church. It is naturally the aim of all preachers to convert those to whom they preach, but the word used in this collective noun had special import during the Reformation. In the fourteenth and first half of the fifteenth century the authority of the Catholic Church over society was absolute. The first statute authorizing the burning of heretics was passed in 1401 so preaching a message that challenged the central tenant of Catholicism

– that God's blessings were channelled through the Pope – meant risking your life. The preachers of the fifteenth century weren't simply trying to convert people to try to bolster the number of followers they had; they were trying to overthrow the doctrine by which whole populations were governed.

A DISCRETION OF PRIESTS

Of all the attributes required of a Catholic priest, discretion is probably considered by the congregation to be the most desirable. Found in *The Book of St Albans* and several other medieval manuscripts, it is one of several collective nouns to describe professions linked to the Church that are ambiguous in their tone.

With Catholicism the dominant religion in the Middle Ages before the Reformation, attending church meant going to confession. At a time when the Devil was perceived to be as real a force as the weather, sinful behaviour was seen as the route to damnation and a guilty conscience was a hard thing to bear. According to Catholic beliefs, the priest had the authority to grant absolution and deliverance from eternal punishment. But this meant telling him everything – and being sincerely sorrowful in your desire to repent. It could be that the use of the word 'discretion' in this group noun is meant in the same ironic tone we see in 'a faith of merchants'. In the small, unchanging communities of the fifteenth century, everybody knew everybody, and unfortunate indiscretions often became fuel for the local gossipmongers. When penitent sinners found that the secrets of the confession box had somehow found their way onto the grapevine, they could only assume that the priest had not been as circumspect as they might have hoped. Less cynically, the noun could be a more literal reference to the discretion practised by the priest as laid out in the 'sacramental seal' – the code of secrecy that a priest had to adhere to on pain of excommunication.

CHAPTER 4

DOMESTIC ANIMALS AND BIRDS

A CLOWDER OR GLARING OF CATS

James Lipton points out the way that this collective noun highlights both the prescriptiveness and the contrariness of some medieval manuscripts, citing first the entry for cats in the Egerton Manuscript of 1450 – 'a clouder of cattys' – beneath which it states 'non dictur a clouster', which he translates as 'one doesn't say cluster'; then turning to the list found at the end of Caxton's print of the 'Horse, Sheep and Goose' which in 1476 pointedly lists 'a cluster of tame cattes'.

In fact, cluster, clowder and clutter probably all had the same roots and could be used interchangeably to describe a group of cats. The *OED* defines cluster as 'a group of similar things or people positioned closely together' and says that it probably comes from *clot*, which stems from the Old English *clott*, meaning a thick mass of material stuck together. Clutter, it says, has Middle English origins 'influenced by cluster'.

Whichever variant you choose, the term perfectly evokes an image of intertwined furry bodies, coiled around each other for warmth and comfort. The alternative noun for cats is just as poetically alluring; the Harley Manuscript lists 'a gloryng of cattis', which Hodgkin explains was interchangeable with *glaryn*, meaning brightly shining, which he feels 'is evidently the proper term to use of a cat's eyes shining in the dark'.

A HERD OR DROVE OF CATTLE

Herd is the most commonly used term of assembly today. It usually refers to a group of grazing animals though it can be applied to any group that acts together without planning or co-ordination. Herds are understood to have formed as a result of the evolutionary advantages gained through having strength in numbers. The stampeding behaviour of grazing animals works in a similar way to the flocking of birds or the forming of fish into a shoal, in that predators are less successful if they are unable to focus their attack on an individual creature.

Humans are believed to have begun to domesticate cattle 10,000 years ago in north-eastern China and cattle farming has been integral to the development of human society ever since. In medieval times, cattle were bred mainly for their meat and milk, but were also used as draft animals. For most of the year medieval cattle herds were left to fend for themselves in the common grazing pastures but in the winter they were brought into barns and fed hay and straw. When they needed to be moved a cattle herd or drover would drive them in from the fields. As beef became the most popular meat of the Middle Ages drovers established trade routes to bring cattle to the growing cities from the lush pastures of the West Country. These were known as drove routes and a herd on the move came to be called a drove.

A BROOD OF CHICKENS

The Book of St Albans lists 'a brood of chickens' and this phrase is still widely used today to describe a number of chicks which hatch together. The word brood comes from the Old English word *brōd*, which has the same roots as the Dutch word *broed* and the German *Brut*, which mean breed. As with many collective nouns for birds it is from the description of a clutch of new hatchlings that the term for the grown bird comes.

Chickens were kept for their eggs and their meat

in medieval England, though their meat wasn't as highly prized as duck or goose. There is evidence that chickens were fattened for the tables of the nobility in a similar way to today, in that they were kept in small coops and fed on high-calorie foods. For peasants, though, eating chicken was less of a regular event; they often kept a few hens for their eggs but wouldn't slaughter the birds until their laying days were over, by which time they were usually on the scrawny side and good only for a stew.

Another collective name for chickens is 'a peep', which has been in use since medieval times to denote the high-pitched call of a chick asking for food.

A RAG OR RAKE OF COLTS

In *The Book of St Albans* the entry is 'a rage of colts', which seems a pleasing fit for the wild, hot-headed nature of young stallions. (For those who aren't fans of horseracing, colts are male horses older than two but not more than four years old.)

Horses were crucial to the medieval hunt and to life in general – being used for everything from transporting supplies of food and building materials to carrying knights into battle – and noble houses kept large numbers of horses of different types and ages. Closer inspection of the other medieval lists, however, suggests that 'rage' was not in fact a nod to the young horses' temperament, but a blend of two other words that appear in alternative manuscripts – rag and rake.

Hodgkin grappled with this one in his search for a rational explanation for the collective name. He found a transcript of a fifteenth-century 'Nominale' or dictionary, which explained the term 'rayke' as a step, and connected it with the Old English word *rayke* or rake, which meant to proceed or go. Eventually he was satisfied by an example given in Brockett's *Glossary* of 1829: 'Rake, the extent of a walk or course. Hence a sheep rake.' From this Hodgkin surmised that 'rake', from which the term rag came, is not from ragged, as perhaps large numbers of galloping and colliding colts might look, or from rage, meaning fury, but instead referred to the track or walk used by the colts on their way from the field to the feeding trough.

A TRIP OF GOATS

Though this group name appears in eighteen different fifteenth-century manuscripts, and also in Gawin Douglas' Scots translation of Virgil's *Aeneidos* published in 1513, its precise etymological origins are uncertain. James Lipton suggests 'trip' might be from the Icelandic *thrypa*, meaning tribe, but I prefer to take as a starting point the origin given by the *OED*, which is the Old French word *tripper*, itself taken from Middle Dutch *trippen*, meaning to skip or hop. In modern English we still use trip to describe quick, light steps, the sort that might be demonstrated by a fleet-footed mountain goat. This source also fits well with the most famous goats in folklore – the Billy Goats Gruff. The Norwegian folktale, collected by Peter Christen Asbjørnsen and Jørgen Moe in 1843, is famous for the line: *'Hvem er det som tripper på mi bru?' skrek trollet.* ('Who's that tripping over my bridge?' said the troll.)

This may be a leap of fantasy too far, but whatever its origins, 'a trip of goats' has established itself as a genuine collective term that even the ultra-strict Hodgkin is happy to accept as a 'proper name' for a herd of goats. The animals were one of the first to be domesticated; the history of goat-herding can be dated back 10,000 years to northern Iran, and in the Middle Ages they were kept for their milk, their meat and their skin, which was used to make flasks for holding water or wine.

A STUD OF HORSES

Horses were at the absolute centre of life in the Middle Ages. They were the only form of transport, they were essential for farming and they carried warriors to war. Rather than the breeds we're familiar with today, medieval horses were classified by the role they played in society. There were destriers, well-bred stallions that could be trained for tournaments and were used as warhorses by royalty and lords; palfreys, bred for general-purpose riding, war and travel, usually owned by the wealthy; coursers, steady cavalry horses; and rouncies, common-grade hack horses of no special breeding.

To ensure a steady supply of horses for these many uses, breeding centres known as stud farms were established. The word stud comes from the Old English *stōd*, which has Germanic origins linked to the German *Stute*, meaning mare. During the Middle Ages, monasteries often ran stud farms and became renowned all over Europe for breeding horses of exceptional pedigree. The Andalusian horse was bred by Carthusian monks in Spain and the Rottaler horse, famous for its role as a warhorse during the Crusades, was bred at a German monastery. State stud farms also existed, the first of which was established under Louis XIV of France in 1665, by which time 'a stud of horses' was already established as the proper collective. Working horses were also referred to as a team or a string, since their lack of breeding meant they hadn't come from a stud.

A PACK OR CRY OR KENNEL OF HOUNDS

Hunting dogs were important members of the medieval household. Every noble family kept kennels for their dogs and these were looked after by a team of dedicated servants, often including a page who would sleep in the kennels with the dogs at night to keep them settled.

There were several company terms that could be applied to a group of hunting dogs. They could be referred to as a pack, or, when their work was done and they were at rest, as a kennel, but a cry of hounds is surely the most poetic. It has been suggested that the noun is a reference to the distinctive baying of hunting dogs when they pick up the scent of their quarry, but the term is more likely to derive from the hunting cry that instructs the hounds in their pursuit. The voice of the huntsman was a crucial tool for connecting him to his dogs as they followed the scent, and vocalisations alongside the sounding of a horn would guide the whole hunt. The traditional English hunting call 'Tally Ho!' is a shortening of 'Tallio, hoix, hark, forward,' which, according to an 1801 edition of *The Sporting Magazine*, is an anglicized version of the French terms *Thia-hilaud* and *a qui forheur*, which appear in *La Vénerie* by Jacques du Fouilloux, first published at Poitiers in 1561. This was adapted into English by George Gascoigne under the title *The Noble Arte of Venerie* and became one of the pillars of a young gentleman's hunting education.

A KINDLE OF KITTENS

This beautifully alliterative group name for kittens appears in *The Book of St Albans* as 'a kyndyll of yonge cattis'. In Middle English *kindelen* meant to give birth to, and probably had its roots in, the Old Norse word of the same meaning: *kynda*. We occasionally use the word as a noun today; vets and cat protection charities still describe a group of kittens as a kindle (though the more generic 'litter' is much more common) and twentieth-century British author Rumer Godden wrote a renowned children's book about a stray cat titled *A Kindle of Kittens*. We also still regularly use the word as a verb, meaning to excite, light up or set something (either literally or metaphorically) aflame. That the phrase is still in use at all today is testament to the far-reaching influence of *The Book of St Albans*, because it is the only medieval list to include the term. The others all feature collective nouns for cats (see 'a clowder of cats') but none mention their young.

Cats were kept as pets in the Middle Ages and were valued as mousers and rat-catchers. This was the age of Dick Whittington who, according to fourteenth-century folk legend, became a rich man when the King of Barbary, whose palace was overrun with mice, paid a fortune to buy his cat. But fear of witchcraft meant that cats were treated with suspicion by many medieval peasants, who believed that they were witches disguising themselves as animals.

A BARREN OF MULES

Mules are the progeny of a male donkey and a female horse. In the Middle Ages they were favoured over either species for hard labour because they combine the patience, sure-footedness and stamina of the donkey with the courage and vigour of the horse.

There are two possible sources of inspiration for this group term for mules. One is the use the animal was put to. Known as a beast of burden, the mule was used for carrying heavy loads, so it's possible that 'barren' comes from bearing, as in load bearing. Supporting this notion is the fact that the first manuscript to list the 'proper names' for groups of animals, the Egerton Manuscript, lists the collective noun for mules as 'a burdynne of mulysse'. References to the animals' carrying capabilities can be found in many early texts, including the Old Testament. It was forbidden for the Israelites to breed one species with another, but they were allowed to use mules and they are often mentioned as riding animals for princes as well as for carrying loads.

The second possibility stems from the animal's genetic inheritance. The cross breeding that produces a mule usually results in infertile offspring; horses have sixty-four chromosomes, donkeys have sixty-two, so mules have sixty-three, which makes reproductive pairing difficult. 'Barren' is a now outdated word for infertile, which was used in reference to people and animals as well as unproductive land, so the group noun could have been a reference to this. A different spelling of the word, baron, is also the name that used to be given to a horse-donkey hybrid where the donkey is the mother.

◆ ◆ ◆

A YOKE OF OXEN

Oxen were one of the most important sources of power in English agricultural history and were used for pulling the metal-tipped ploughs that prepared the fields for crop planting. In his instructional poem 'Five Hundred Pointeth of Good Husbandrie', published in 1573, English poet and farmer Thomas Tusser details what was needed at ploughing time:

Two ploughs and a plough chein,
two culters, three shares,
With ground cloutes & side clouts
for soile that so tares:
With ox bowes and oxyokes,
and other things mo,
For oxteeme and horseteeme,
in plough for to go.

A yoke refers to a pair of oxen, bearing a yoke – a wooden frame strapped across the shoulders of the animals and fastened to a plough. The yoke kept the animals in pace with each other and also helped the farmer to control the animals, since the weight of one ox would act as a brake on the other. Oxen were usually paired young and trained together, so that after several years working together they became closely bonded and could often be seen grazing side by side long after the yoke had been taken off. Biblical references to a 'yoke of oxen' helped cement this group name's place in the public consciousness at a time when most people relied on the land for their livelihoods. The King James Bible tells of Elisha 'the son of Shaphat, who was plowing with twelve yoke of oxen before him, and he with the twelfth: and Elijah passed by him, and cast his mantle upon him.'

A FLOCK OF SHEEP

'A flock of shepe' is included in the list at the back of Caxton's 1477 printing of John Lydgate's poem 'Horse, Sheep and Goose' and appears on most of the medieval lists. Along with herd it is probably the most widely used collective noun in modern times and it's hard to believe that it shares its early printed sources with the now obsolete likes of a clowder of cats, a labour of moles and a mutation of thrushes.

Its endurance probably owes much to the complete overhaul of the countryside that occurred shortly after the lists of collective nouns were recorded, also known as enclosure. During the sixteenth century, landowners with large manorial estates began unilaterally to enclose land that had previously been used for arable farming and turn it into pasture for sheep grazing. The increased demand for English wool abroad made this a far more profitable enterprise than growing crops. But as the lords of the manor grew richer, the peasants grew poorer. Without agricultural work, many people found themselves destitute and left the towns and villages their families had lived in for generations. Finding the village buildings empty, sheep-farming lords knocked them down to make way for yet more pasture and the cycle continued. By 1533 the situation was so bad that Henry VIII supported a statute limiting the size of flock a landlord could own to 2,000 animals. Epigram 20 of English clergyman Thomas Bastard sums up the popular view in his 1598 collection *Chrestoleros*:

> *Shepe have eate up our meadow*
> *and our downes,*
> *Our corne, our wood, our villages*
> *and townes.*

A DRIFT OF TAME SWINE

The Book of St Albans distinguishes tame swine from the wild, since wild swine were a valued beast of the hunt and described in terms hunters would use (see 'a sounder of wild swine'), while tame pigs were referred to with the language of the farmer or herder. In eighteenth-century author Thomas Wright's

Volume of Vocabularies, which examines language spoken between the tenth and fifteenth centuries, drift is defined as 'a driving of beasts'.

Domesticated pigs were tended to by a swineherd, who looked after them in much the same way a shepherd tends his flock. In medieval times pig farmers were permitted to let their animals roam free in the forests of the manorial estate for a part of the year. When the forest acorns and beechnuts

ripened and fell in early autumn, the swineherds would drive the pigs into these woodlands for a period of six weeks to forage for them. This process was known as pannaging and a peasant had to pay a small fee for 'pannage rights'. However, the nut-rich diet worked well to fatten the swine, which would usually be ready for slaughter in mid-November.

Pork was an important contribution to the diet of better-off medieval families and every part of the animal was used. A portion of the flesh was roasted and eaten fresh, leaving plenty to be salted and smoked so it would last for the whole winter. The blood was drained and saved for black puddings and the skin was turned into leather.

A RAFTER OF TURKEYS

In *An Exaltation of Larks* James Lipton points out the ease with which the origins of this noun could be mistakenly linked to the wooden rafters of barn roofs. It seems to make sense – turkeys do have an instinctive desire to perch overnight to keep them safe from ground-level predators – but this rafter isn't the same roof beam we know it as today.

The *OED* explains that the word originates from 'raft', which can be defined as 'a dense flock of swimming birds or mammals: great rafts of cormorants, often 5,000 strong.' And which the *Webster Dictionary* defines as 'a large and often motley collection of people and things, as a raft of books'. A flock of turkeys, gobbling and scratching the earth, might well be described as a motley collection.

Turkeys are so named because early European explorers of the New World believed they were related to guinea fowl, which were introduced to medieval Europe from Turkey and nicknamed turkey fowl.

CHAPTER 5

WILD ANIMALS, INSECTS AND FISH

A CETE OF
BADGERS

The Middle English word for badger was grey or
gray, from their greyish appearance under moonlight,
and 'a cete of grayis' appears in *The Book of St Albans*
and several other lists. Many collective nouns that
appear in the early manuscripts are derived from
the animal's habitat ('an earth of foxes', 'a drey of
squirrels') and it's tempting to link this 'cete' to the
sett we now know of as the badger's home – an
underground network of tunnels and chambers built
into sloping ground in woodland.

Complicating this theory, though, is the fact that
the Egerton Manuscript uses 'a syght' of badgers.
Syght meant sight, and Hodgkin insists that since

badgers have never been known for their eyesight this must have been a transcriber's mistake. The animals were believed to possess magical powers, however, and as creatures of the night were thought by some to have prophetic powers – sometimes known as 'second sight' – as this eighteenth-century rhyme shows:

Should one hear a badger call,
And then an ullot cry,
Make thy peace with God, good soul,
For thou shall shortly die.

Unlike other vermin, badgers weren't especially prized by the medieval hunt. In the fourteenth-century *Livre de Chasse* (*Book of the Hunt*), Gaston Phoebus notes that the badger's short legs, fatty bodies and fetid odour meant they were not considered fair game, though later the dachshund was bred in Germany specifically to rout out the animal, its name translating as 'badger-dog'.

Whatever the inspiration behind the collective noun it stuck and was given by Coles' *An English Dictionary* in 1685 and Cocker's *English Dictionary* in 1715 as 'a company of badgers'.

A SWARM OF BEES

Just as herd and flock have become catch-all collective terms for animals and birds, swarm is used to describe massed insects of all varieties, but it was for bees that the word was used first. It comes from the Old English *swearm*, meaning multitude, and the *OED* records its use from the early fifteenth century to describe a large, dense throng. There could be no better word to describe a bee colony in flight and 'swarming' has become an established term to describe the method by which honey-bee colonies reproduce.

When a colony is at its largest and beginning to outgrow its hive, it produces another queen and half the colony depart in search of a new home; they often choose hollow trees, cracks in walls and abandoned manmade hives to set up in. The swarm is so dense because all the worker bees stay clustered around the queen.

Bee-keeping has been practised since the early civilizations, and Domesday entries reveal that in England's cooler climate, medieval bee-keepers often practised 'swarm beekeeping', which meant keeping bees in smaller hives called skeps, made from coiled wicker, to encourage early swarming. As the old queen and her house-hunting colony set off, the beekeeper would follow on foot until they settled and he could get them into his skep in time for the honey-making season. The sooner they swarmed the better, as this old English rhyme reveals:

A swarm of bees in May is
worth a load of hay;
A swarm of bees in June is
worth a silver spoon;
A swarm of bees in July
isn't worth a fly.

A LITTER OF CUBS

The word cub can be used to describe the young of foxes, bears, lions, leopards and wolves, and the word litter applies to a number of any of these animals' cubs born to a mother at one time, as well as to puppies and kittens. Its origin is Middle English and according to the *OED* it comes from the medieval Latin word *lectaria*, from the Latin *lectus*, meaning bed. As a collective noun this one is still in regular use today and may have enjoyed such longevity because of its everyday applications for domesticated animals.

It appears in several of the medieval manuscripts and in those days would have most frequently been used by huntsmen to describe wolf cubs. Wolves were designated by the English aristocracy as one of five 'Royal Beasts of the Chase' and in spite of their foul smell, their pelts were prized for use as scarves and mittens. There was also an extra pride to be taken for killing a wolf because they were seen as evil creatures. They'd been hunted enthusiastically since the thirteenth century when King Edward I ordered their complete extermination in the Midlands and by 1427 King James I of Scotland had enshrined the need for three wolf hunts a year in law, specifying that these should take place during the wolves' cubbing season. This was probably because wolves upped their stealthy attacks on sheep folds when they had hungry cubs to feed. It was this threat the wolf posed to the livelihoods of farmers that gave them their sinister reputation, cemented by the folklore that if a wolf lays eyes on a man before the man sees him, the man will be unable to speak.

A HERD OF DEER

Of all the creatures that were hunted for sport in the Middle Ages, the deer was the top prize. The animals' speed and agility made them a challenge for the most experienced of huntsman and the deliciousness of their meat was an added enticement.

The word herd was applied to all deer: hert, hynde, bucks and does. (Only roe deer were omitted and instead were collectively called 'a bevvy of roos'.) For the uninitiated, herts are how stags used to be described, hynde refers specifically to female red deer, bucks are smaller male deer and a doe, as *The Sound of Music* teaches us, is a deer, a female deer. These distinctions were basic hunting knowledge for anyone attempting to pass themselves off as a gentleman, but it was just as important to know whether to call the herd you were hunting a little, middle or large herd. Dame Juliana Barnes, the fourteenth-century English writer on hawking, heraldry and hunting, had a helpful rhyme to recite if remembering the rules proved tricky in the heat of the chase. The 'XX', 'XL' and 'LXXX' refer to Roman numerals.

XX is a littyll herd though
it be of hyndes
And XL is a mydyle herde
to call hym be kyndis
And LXXX is a grete herde.
Call ye hem so
Be it hert be it hynde
bucke or el lis doo.

A BUSYNESS OF FERRETS

For catching rabbits, the best weapon in the armoury of the medieval huntsman was the ferret. Like hawking, ferreting was a popular pastime for the well-to-do, but it was also an illicit means to a good meal for the peasant. In Gaston Phoebus' 1380s *Livre de Chasse* (or *Book of the Hunt*) there is a plate showing a hunting scene in which muzzled ferrets are being put down rabbit holes to chase the rabbits out of their burrows and into the purse nets at the warren's other exits. A similar scene is depicted in 'The Ferreter's Tapestry', a fifteenth-century tapestry from Burgundy in France.

As hunting companions, ferrets were prized for their speed and tenacity and this collective noun pays tribute to their businesslike way of carrying out their work. 'Busyness' appears in many of the medieval lists as a group name for ferrets, but this is an interesting example of the Chinese-whisper effect in print. As many of the manuscripts listing the proper names for groups of animals were copied from previous lists, errors occasionally crept in and, when they did, they were often perpetuated by later compilers. Antiquarian and writer Joseph Strutt made one of the more well-known modern collections in his *Sports and Pastimes of the People of England*, published in 1801, but he made a simple typographical error

– in his volume 'besynes' became 'fesynes' – and readers without access to his source material took his version as fact. Several modern-day collectors of group nouns have mistakenly used 'fesynes' and so the error has been passed on.

A SHOAL OF FISH

Just as herd has become the natural way to describe a group of animals, and flock a group of birds, any mass of fish is described as either a school, or a shoal. The closeness of the spellings has led to a belief that they are variations of the same word, and in his 1909 examination of medieval collective nouns John Hodgkin adhered to this view, insisting that school is simply a variant spelling of shoal.

However, in his book on the subject, James Lipton sides with twentieth-century lexicographer Eric Partridge, who identifies different roots for the two words: school coming from the Middle English *scole*, which stems from the Latin word for school – *schola*, and shoal coming via the Old English *sceald*, meaning shallow. Yet another source is suggested by the *OED*, which gives the Middle Dutch *schōle*, meaning 'troop' as the source of both school and shoal. The definitive answer is lost in the labyrinth of time but there's no denying that 'a shallows of fish' feels in keeping with the rest of the terms of venery listed in the medieval manuscripts.

There's also something whimsical about the word that suits the sea, as Milton demonstrates in Book Seven of *Paradise Lost*, when he has God say:

> *Forthwith the sounds and seas,*
> *each creek and bay,*
> *With fry innumerable swarm,*
> *and shoals*
> *Of fish that, with their fins*
> *and shining scales,*
> *Glide under the green wave*
> *in sculls that oft*
> *Bank the mid-sea.*

A SKULK OF FOXES

This is an example of how enigmatic the true origins of many of the oldest terms of multitude can be. Were the creators of early lists inspired by an animal's habits or by its habitat? This one seems surely to have its roots in the behaviour of the fox, which is known for its stealth and cunning – its skulking movements. Medieval folklore had already made people familiar with the craftiness of foxes through the character of Reynard or Reynardine, the sly fox of French folk tales. His wily ways became well known in England after William Caxton, founder of the country's first printing press, translated the stories into English in 1481.

Skulking can also be defined as lying in hiding or keeping out of sight, which one might imagine would be appropriate behaviour for a fox that is being pursued by an aristocratic hunt on horseback. But at least one of the medieval manuscripts to list collective nouns has 'a sulk of foxes', instead of 'a skulk', which suggests an alternative explanation. The missing letter could simply have been an error at the printing press, of course, but some scholars have tentatively put forward the possibility that 'sulk' could be derived from the Latin *sulcus*, meaning ditch or furrow, which would link the noun to the foxes' home – an earth. Indeed, some medieval lists use 'an earth of foxes' as the correct collective noun.

A CLOUD OF GNATS

One of the most literally descriptive of the collective nouns from the medieval lists, this is still in regular use today, conveying so neatly the quietly humming sphere of small flies that can often be seen at dusk in summer time. Unlike many other winged creatures, gnats can't really be classified as a swarm because they don't form groups in order to go anywhere. They're not on the lookout for a new home, like a swarm of bees, or foraging for food, like a swarm of ants.

Gnats don't have time for such behaviour; in adult form they live for only five to seven days. They pupate, they hover, they mate and then they die. It's a life span that necessitates speed and practicality when it comes to reproduction, so gnats have evolved methods to allow males and females to find each other easily in their marsh and woodland homes. Males hover together over an easily identifiable object where they wait for a female to spot them. Then they cluster around the female, using her pheromones to keep them as close to her as possible, which is what creates the distinctive ball-shaped appearance of the cloud.

Edmund Spenser describes a gentle shepherd walking through a gnat cloud in *The Faerie Queen*:

A Cloud of cumbrous
Gnats do him molest,
All striving to infix their
feeble Stings,
That from their noyance
he no where can rest,
He brushes oft, and oft
doth mar their Mumurings.

A HUSK OF HARES

This pleasingly alliterative group name is something of an enigma. There's no obvious link between hares and the word husk, which means the outer shell or coating of a seed, and there are no

archaic definitions of the word to offer any other interpretation. The ever-careful Hodgkin finds 'nothing can be said with certainty – Dr Bradley suspects some scribal error, which the later lists have copied', though there are no clues as to what the mistaken scribe might have meant to write.

We'll have to be satisfied with knowing that someone, at some time in the 1400s, thought that a husk of hares had a certain rural ring to it, and for me that's good enough. There are other options, though. The Egerton Manuscript has 'a drove of hare', which is a reference to the way they were driven from their burrows when hunted. Certainly, hares were highly valued as the most noble of quarries. Hare coursing using greyhounds was popular because of the sustained length of the chase and the fact that unlike animals of chase, the hare could be hunted all year round. Their pelts were also prized and special methods were used to prevent their coats from being spoiled.

In Gaston Phoebus' *Book of the Hunt*, written in 1387, he describes the different arrows used for hunting and explains that sharp iron points were used for hunting bears, wild boars and stags, while for hunting hare, the arrows had a large, club-like end made from lead, which was designed to stun the animal without piercing its body.

A RICHESSE OF MARTENS

The European pine marten was considered a top prize for hunters in the Middle Ages. Of all the 'vermin of the chase', which included foxes, wild cats, polecats and squirrels, the marten was the most sought after because hunters could charge a substantial price for their pelts. In his examination of the terms of venery in *The Book of St Albans*, Hodgkin refers us to a book by sixteenth-century English cleric Edward Topsell called *The History of Four-footed Beasts*, which says: 'A hunter that hath killed a Martin ... cannot chuse but bee very joyful which get a good sum of a money for a little labour as they have for a martin's skin.'

Less readily available furs were worn by the royal family and members of the nobility. Tudor 'statutes of apparel' – strict laws governing the amount of money the people could spend on clothing – dictated the colours, cuts and materials that could be worn by each level of society and stated which furs could be worn by which tier of the aristocracy. Only those of or above the rank of duke, marquise and earl were allowed to wear sable fur, which came from the luxurious coat of the Siberian weasel; ermine, the white winter coat of the stoat, which could only be obtained for a few months of the year, was reserved for royalty. Fur from animals outside the King or Queen's dominion was only allowed to be worn by those with an income of at least £100 a year, while anyone below the rank of a serving man was not allowed to wear fur at all.

A LABOUR OF MOLES

Moles are solitary creatures, coming together only to mate, so it would be a rare thing to see a company of moles, but the creature's habits certainly lend themselves to this collective name. Moles dig for about four hours at a time, then rest for about the same period, before starting to dig again. They feed on earthworms and insects that live in surface soil, using their network of tunnels just as spiders use their webs to catch their food. The animals' large, spade-like forepaws allow them to dig up to 20 metres of tunnel and shovel 540 times their own body weight in soil, every single day.

In medieval times the mole's life of hard labour was well understood. Their shallow tunnels often caused the roots of vegetables to dry out and most villages had a mole catcher, who could also make money from selling the pelts of the creatures he caught to make warm moleskin waistcoats and trousers.

In Middle English the mole was also called a moldwarp or moldiwarp, from 'mold' meaning earth and 'warp' meaning throw. English poet John Clare describes the mole catcher's harvest in his poems against enclosure:

O I never call to mind
These pleasant names of places
but I leave a sigh behind
While I see the little mouldiwarps
hang sweeing to the wind
On the only aged willow that in all
the field remains.

A HOVER OF TROUT

This noun is based on the trout's tendency to hover just below the surface of the water. It's a surprisingly accurate description; trout have a swim bladder – a flotation device that they fill by coming to the surface of the water and taking a gulp of air. This inflates and allows the fish to hold a position at a particular depth. To sink lower the trout simply burps out bubbles of air.

Stream-dwelling trout don't need to swim around after their prey: instead they lie in wait, 'hovering' at a good vantage point known as a 'lie' and watch for insects to feed on. When they spot something they dart out and swallow it before returning to the lie to wait again. During the summer when insects are plentiful, trout often hover just beneath the surface of the water with their mouths open, allowing the steady flow of nutritious food to flow in. In his book *The Language of Field Sports*, C. E. Hare describes 'a hover of trout' as a shoal of trout 'waiting on the edge of fast water in great numbers ready to dash at food brought down by the stream'.

Trout was often mentioned in medieval cookery books and was most commonly served with the 'Verde sawse' (green sauce) described here: 'Take parsel, garlek, a litul serpell ans sawge, a litul canel, gynger, piper, wyne, brede, vyneger & salt; boile and grynge it smal and messe it forth.'

For banquets they were often served 'swimming', which meant they were presented as whole fish, heads and tails intact, top to tail as if hovering in the green sauce.

A ROUT OF WOLVES

Though we've grown used to referring to a group of wolves as a pack, several of the medieval manuscripts insist upon rout. The word was first used in the Middle Ages and can be traced to the Latin word *ruptus*, meaning broken. We now most often use it as a verb – to rout a pack of wolves would be to cause them to retreat – but in the fifteenth century the *OED* explains that it was used to describe 'a disorderly or tumultuous crowd of people'.

Wolves were a popular animal to hunt in the Middle Ages and the animal's stamina and wiliness were a particular draw for ambitious huntsmen. Their place near the top of the hierarchy of hunted animals is illustrated by their inclusion in a rhyme from *The Book of St Albans*:

> *My chylde callith herdys*
> *of hert and of hynde*
> *And of Bucke and of Doo*
> *where yo hem finde*
> *And a Beue of Roos what*
> *place they be in*
> *And a sounder ye shall of*
> *the wylde swine*
> *And a Rowte of wolues*
> *where they passin inne*
> *So shall ye hem call as*
> *many as they bene.*

CHAPTER 6

WILD BIRDS

A BELLOWING OF BULLFINCHES

If you're unfamiliar with the song of the bullfinch you could be forgiven for assuming from this group name that it was loud and low. But in fact the bullfinch is thought to have got its name from its appearance rather than its call. The *OED* remarks that 'some have suggested that it was given on account of the thickness of the bird's neck'.

In medieval times the bird's name was in fact shortened to simply 'bull', and since the bullfinch's song is in fact quiet and warbling, it is clearly from the bird's four-footed namesake that the noun originates. Bullfinches were considered a pest of fruit crops and were singled out in a 1566 act against 'noysome fowles' and vermin which declared that 'everie Bulfynche and other byrde that devoureth the blowth [bud] of the fruit' would have a price of 1d upon its head. This seems especially cruel in light of the bird's decline in recent years, but at the time they were a threat to the survival of the rural population. The fruit crops grown in the hedgerows across rural England were a crucial source of food and income for country dwellers and the bullfinches' voracious appetite posed a serious threat to this. During the hungry winter months they descend on fruit trees in great numbers and a single bird can easily devour up to thirty buds a minute.

A COVERT OF COOTS

We're used to the meaning of covert, since though French in origin – from *couvert* meaning to cover or conceal – it's a word we have long since adopted into the English language. International news is full of covert operations, missions carried out secretly under the cover of darkness to avoid detection.

Often the collective nouns listed in *The Book of St Albans* and other medieval compilations are derived from observations of the animals' natural characteristics, so we might be forgiven for assuming from the group name given to them that coots must display some natural hiding skills. Not so. The coot in fact parades around in the open on its long legs, its distinctive white beak marking it out for all to see. It also has one of the most conspicuous nests of any water bird, building a stack of twigs and branches half a metre high, often in the middle of a lake or stream. Their inability to defend their young by making any kind of concealment for the nest has resulted in them developing excellent abilities as lookouts, but covert in their behaviour they are not.

This noun instead has its roots in the name given to the group of new hatchlings, who are concealed beneath their mother as she sits on the nest. The term may have begun as a description of a group of young coots or coot chicks and then been applied to the species in general.

A MURDER OF CROWS

This unusual name for a flock of crows appeared in many of the early manuscripts as a 'murther of crowes' – from *murthre*, the Middle English word for murder. While most terms for groups of birds are linked to their song or habitat, this one has its roots in bird behaviour and medieval folklore. With their dark feathers and jet-black eyes, crows were regarded by fifteenth-century peasants as sinister creatures of the night. Along with other corvids such as ravens and rooks they were believed to be messengers of the Devil or witches in disguise. They were also suspected of having prophetic powers and the appearance of a crow on the roof of a house was taken as an omen that someone inside would soon die.

The crow's association with death was enhanced by its habits. They are scavengers, often feeding on the carcasses of dead animals and gathering in great numbers over battlefields or near sick livestock. There are also stories of the birds enacting something known as a crow parliament (*kråkriksdag* in Swedish) during which up to 500 birds are said to gather together in the branches of trees or on open ground and caw at each other for a while before suddenly setting upon one of their number and tearing it to pieces with their claws and beaks. Ornithologists confirm that crows are highly intelligent, teaching their young to use tools and sometimes even ganging together to attack predators.

A HERD OF CURLEW

The curlew is the largest British wading bird and this term appears in *The Book of St Albans* and on other fifteenth-century lists. Modern bird watchers may wince but at that time curlew formed a regular part of a nobleman's diet. One medieval recipe 'for to boil pheasant, partridges, capons and curlews' suggests the meat had gamey qualities and gives simple instructions for its preparation: 'Take a good broth and add the fowl to this then add whole peppercorns and plenty of grounned cinnamon and let them boil

with then serve it forth and sprinkle over powder douce.'

Curlew congregate in large numbers all around Britain's coastline. They feed using their characteristic long downward-curving bill to probe deep into damp ground, though they don't keep exclusively to marshland: large flocks can often be seen standing in fields and meadows, dotted at regular intervals across the landscape. In the colder months in particular, wintering birds might take to permanent pastures to feed on earthworms and insects they find in the soil, which may be why they came to be described as a herd.

◆　◆　◆

A PADDLING OF DUCKS (ON WATER)

The Book of St Albans lists this as 'a badelynge of dokis', which may have been a misprint. Many of the entries in Dame Juliana's list also appear on the earlier handwritten manuscripts and this one can be found in the Egerton Manuscript as a 'padelynge'. In the ornate gothic script used by scribes in the 1400s a 'p' could quite easily have been mistaken for a 'b', and since the Egerton proves that paddling was already a word associated with ducks on water it seems likely that the change is simply a misreading or a typographical mistake.

There are in fact several collective nouns to describe a flock of ducks, all usefully applicable to the different environments in which they might be observed. On land they're often referred to as 'a safe', possibly because they were protected from the hawks used by noble huntsmen as long as they kept close to the ground. Other terms applied once the ducks were flushed into the air (see 'a sord or suit of mallards' and 'a spring of teal').

Historian Richard Almond's book *Medieval Hunting* describes how hunting ducks was particularly popular with 'lady falconers', who used a method known as 'flying at the brook', in which he explains 'falcons were flown at herons or wild duck, flushed and put up by pointers or spaniels'. He also refers to the several illuminations from fourteenth- and fifteenth-century psalters and prayer books that show ducks being hunted. In one instance a noble lady sounds a gong beside a duck on water (a solitary duck, rather than a paddling) in order to flush it so her falcon could catch it mid-flight.

A FLING OF DUNLINS

Like many group names for birds, this one takes inspiration from the birds' flight. Dunlin flocks are usually large, often made up of up to fifty individuals, and when they're being hunted by peregrine falcons and merlins, their natural predators in the wild as well as in medieval hunting, they have a distinctive flying pattern involving highly co-ordinated aerial manoeuvres. Moving as one, the birds tack and wheel, at one moment a dense mass of white belly feathers, at the next a block of pale grey wings. Their flight is fast and erratic, zig-zagging urgently across the sky, sometimes landing simultaneously and a second later taking flight again, always tightly packed together to present themselves as an impenetrable body to the circling hawks.

This characteristic flight pattern fits well with our modern use of the word 'fling' as descriptive of a forceful throw or violent, sudden movement, which dates back to Middle English use. The *OED* suggests the word may have its roots in the Old Norse word *flengia*, meaning 'flog'. It's a collective name that is likely to have been regularly used in practice because dunlins were a target of the medieval hunt. They were often hunted by noblewomen, who used merlins as hawking birds. Prized as many water birds were for their meat, they were sometimes served as part of a 'twelve-bird roast' – where one bird is stuffed inside another and so on – for a Christmas feast.

A SKEIN OF GEESE (IN THE AIR)

A skein is used instead of a gaggle when a flock of geese is in flight. The word has been in use since around 1400 and is a shortening of the Old French *escaigne*, which meant a hank of yarn. A hank or skein of yarn is a long length of yarn folded back on itself in a shape similar to the 'v' formation that airborne geese fly in when they travel long distances.

For flying geese, the 'v' is critical for ensuring they can endure their migratory flights. It works by allowing the geese further back in the formation to ride on the updrafts created by the wings of the bird in front. When the lead goose gets tired, it moves to the back and another member of the flock takes its place. Geese can fly 70 per cent further in this way than if they were making the journey alone. Other collective nouns for flying geese include a team or a wedge, both of which make reference to this same distinctive group-flying tactic.

In American environmentalist Aldo Leopold's 1949 book, *A Sand County Almanac*, his March entry includes the following poetic lines:

> *One swallow does not make a summer, but one skein of geese, cleaving the murk of a March thaw, is the spring.*

A GAGGLE OF GEESE (ON LAND)

Ask someone to think of an example of a collective noun and nine times out of ten they'll give you this one. It's something we learn in childhood and we accept it in the same easy way that we accept flock and herd as generic group names for other birds and grazing animals. It appears alongside all the others included in this book on the fifteenth-century manuscripts and yet in contrast to so many of the others, it has found a genuine place in everyday parlance.

The 1702 *New English Dictionary* sums up the situation regarding the origins and uses of collective nouns in its entry for 'a gaggle of geese', describing it as 'one of the many artificial terms invented in the fifteenth century as distinctive collectives referring to particular animals or classes of persons; but unlike most of the others, it seems to have been actually adopted in use'.

Its absorption into real language may be linked to its alliterative appeal. The words roll off the tongue and therefore establish themselves in the subconscious more readily than other less memorable group nouns. In 1607 Stephen Skinner included the term in his etymologicon *Linguae Anglicanae* under 'noises of birds' and described it as coming from the sounds geese make to each other while waddling along. Gaggle is also used, some may feel unfairly, as a collective noun for women.

A CHARM OF GOLDFINCHES

This noun can be found in its earlier form – 'a chirme' or 'a chirming of goldfinches' – in many of the manuscripts of the Middle Ages, though they are also occasionally referred to as 'a glister', meaning glitter. Goldfinches were a popular cage bird and were a regular target of hawkers, who were members of the aristocracy who hunted using birds of prey. As a result they are mentioned in most of the lists of hunting terms that guided the nobility in the proper way of referring to hunted prey.

In the sixteenth century, 'chirm' became 'charm' and the name is still widely used in its updated form today. The durability of its appeal owes much to the fact that modern users misunderstand its meaning. Goldfinches are tiny and pretty and we find them charming, so it feels right to describe a group of them as 'a charm'. In fact though, 'charm' had a different meaning in medieval times. In those days it meant simply to chirp, or make a noise like a bird. 'Chirm' and then 'charm' referred specifically to the chattering, trilling song characteristic of finches, which intermingles to create a confused hum or clamour when many finches sing together.

The noun appears with poetic resonance in reference to non-specific singing birds in the Garden of Eden in Book Four of Milton's *Paradise Lost*:

Sweet is the breath of morn,
her rising sweet,
With charm of earliest birds.

A CAST OF HAWKS

Hawking was a section of the medieval hunt that really underlined the supremacy of the upper echelons of the aristocracy. Owning and training birds of prey took money and only the wealthiest landowners could afford to employ highly skilled falconers.

The fashion for falconry took hold in England around the middle of the eighth century, when Ethelbert, King of Kent, was presented with a hawk and two falcons. It quickly became a highly esteemed sport and proficiency in hawking was considered an essential quality in gentlemen of rank across the country. Books explaining the detailed rules of hawking were part of the education of the elite classes; one third of *The Book of St Albans* is devoted to it and it is explicit about the importance of the language surrounding hawking. In one particularly prescriptive section it states: 'Ye shall say *cast* the hawk ether to, and not *let fli it* ther to.' There were also strict rules about the type of bird that each member of the nobility should use when hawking, also detailed in *The Book of St Albans*. The King should fly a gyr falcon (male and female), a prince should have a peregrine falcon, dukes had rock falcons, earls had male tiercel peregrine falcons, barons bastarde hawks, ladies could fly female merlins and yeomen a goshawk or hobby. Knaves, servants and children could only use kestrels.

The 1702 *New English Dictionary* explains that 'a cast of hawks' refers to 'the number of hawks cast off [released by a falconer] at a time: a couple', though this is only used in reference to the so-called Hawks of the Tower. Those used by the aristocracy were referred to as 'a cast', whereas a pair or more of mere goshawks was called 'a flight'.

A SIEGE OF HERONS

Medieval warfare was usually waged by laying siege to a town or castle. Walled cities well stocked with provisions and served by a network of tunnels for the supply of fresh water could withstand an assault for months, but if the attacking army had the strength and patience to sit tight, the city would eventually fall. The medieval castles that survive today reveal in their construction the need to be able to withstand siege warfare, with their high walls, moats, arrow slits and murder holes through which boiling oil could be poured on advancing enemies.

Though the long-legged heron seems like a peaceful creature, there are good reasons for 'a siege' to be used in describing a group of them. Written as 'a sege of herons' in *The Book of St Albans*, the word siege came from the Latin *sedere*, meaning to sit, and it was used in the Middle Ages as a collective noun for herons because of the bird's hunting methods. Herons sit on their nest or stand, one-legged, in the water, completely motionless, until a fish passes, oblivious to the predator waiting to pounce. Once the fish is in reach, the heron brings down its bill and plucks the fish from the water and so medieval hunting guides describe the heron sitting on the riverbank as being 'at siege'. It's one of the many collective nouns for animals and birds that were inspired by observation of the creatures' behaviour and yet it also sheds light on a tumultuous and violent passage in our history.

A DECEIT OF
LAPWINGS

This appears in *The Book of St Albans* and subsequent lists of collective nouns as 'a desserte', which translates into modern English as merit or worthiness. But in the Egerton Manuscript, which preceded *St Albans*, it was written as 'dyssayte', which is equivalent to the modern word deceit. This version is thought to be correct as it takes inspiration from the natural behaviour of the bird when threatened.

Lapwings are waders that build their nests on the bare ground or in short vegetation on farmland or marshes. The nest is usually just a scrape in the sand or mud so the only protection the birds have is the ability to see potential predators as they approach. Lapwings also move their chicks from the nesting site to habitation more suitable for chick-rearing shortly after they hatch and the young birds are very vulnerable during this move. To defend their brood, lapwings will mob predators to scare them away, but the birds are also known for using distraction techniques as a means of defending their young. They've been found fiercely protecting a decoy nest and parent birds will hop on one leg with their wing extended as if broken to entice predators away from their chicks. Indeed, some sources suggest that their name comes from this characteristic broken-wing performance.

Chaucer's dream-vision poem 'The Parliament

of Fowls' gives an insight into the reputation these tactics gave the bird in the late 1300s, describing it as 'the false lapwing, ful of threcherie'. Hodgkin also notes that the French country term for lapwing is *dix-huit*, in an imitation of its call, and speculates that the English word 'deceit' might be used in a punning way.

AN EXALTATION OF LARKS

The early eighteenth-century *New English Dictionary* describes this as 'a fanciful name for a flight of larks' and it is certainly one of the most whimsical and poetic. The *OED* defines exaltation as both a feeling or state of extreme happiness and the action of praising someone or something highly. In this case the lark could be said to be both full of joy and praising the natural world with its song.

A single lark's ascension into the sky while in full song was traditionally known as an exaltation and sometime in the thirteenth or early fourteenth century it was put to use as a collective noun. Indeed, this term was selected by American writer, actor and television producer James Lipton for the title of his quintessential collection of real and invented group terms, first published in 1968. In it he explains, under the entry 'an exultation of fireworks', that he received many letters asking him why the phrase in his title was *exaltation* and not *exultation* (meaning a feeling of triumphant, upsurging elation). Both words were in use when the terms were written down in the Middle Ages but, as Lipton himself puts it, 'the codifiers, without exception, chose exaltation, which can have either the sense of praising (the sky, the moment, life) or of an exalted state'.

Shakespeare makes moving use of the exalting lark in Sonnet 29, likening its accent to the way the spirits can be lifted by love after a period of melancholy:

> *Haply I think on thee, and then my state,*
> *Like to the lark at break of day arising*
> *From sullen earth, sings hymns at heaven's gate.*

A TIDING OF MAGPIES

Superstition permeated all aspects of life in the Middle Ages. The brutality of medieval survival and the hovering spectre of premature death drove people to put as much faith in omens, magic and supernatural forces as they did in God. Everyday occurrences were read as signs of good or bad luck to come and the natural world was analysed for clues as to what might lie ahead.

Magpies in particular were believed to have potent prophetic powers and the tidings they brought determined whether you'd find happiness or despair. Their message was thought to be found in the number of birds that appeared in a flock; a lone magpie was always the harbinger of doom. According to Christian folklore, the magpie was the only bird not to sing to Jesus as he suffered on the cross, which gave it a reputation for meanness amongst the god-fearing peasantry. It was also believed in some areas to hold a drop of the Devil's blood beneath its tongue, and any creature bound to the Devil was to be deeply feared. In larger numbers, though, the bird could impart less sinister tidings, as the following old rhyme reveals:

One for sorrow,
Two for joy,
Three for a girl,
Four for a boy,
Five for silver,
Six for gold,
Seven for a secret,
never to be told.

A tiding of magpies works especially well as a collective noun because a flock of them was always seen as bringing news of some kind.

A SORD OR SUIT OF MALLARDS

In the midst of the poetry of these ancient collective nouns, it's easy to drift away from the fact that the original set of terms applied directly to animals that were to be hunted is referred to in all the early pieces of writing on hunting as 'terms of venery'. Nowadays we associate the word venery with physical love but its roots are in the Latin word *venari*, meaning to hunt game. The terms that were most strictly adhered to were those that applied to game birds and animals that were commonly hunted in Europe.

With such roots, it's little wonder that many of

the terms relate to the reaction of a bird or animal when it is disturbed. A hunting team stalking the marshland at the edge of a great estate would be on the lookout for creatures that had been flushed from their hiding places. If they'd seen a flock of mallards taking to the air they would have described them as a sord, from *soudre*, the Old French word meaning to spring, which in turn came from the Latin *surgere*, to surge. It's descriptive of the way that mallards take flight by springing up from the water. Sometimes the term found in the medieval lists is 'a suit of mallards', and this seems to come from the French *suite*, or Old French *suitte*, meaning following one after another, which is exactly how mallards order themselves when they've been routed. Other manuscripts suggest 'a flush of mallards' for just the same reasons.

A WATCH OF NIGHTINGALES

Nightingales are named for their characteristic behaviour of singing long into the night. While most birds sing at dusk and then rest before beginning again at dawn, the male nightingale frequently delivers its beautiful song during the hours of darkness, in the hopes of attracting a mate. The term 'watch' in this context may have its roots in an archaic definition of the word meaning to stay awake at night in order to practise some religious observance, as the bird's melodious tones have often been compared to a rejoicing hymn. But another use of the word that is still current could in fact be the source. A watch can also be defined as a period of keeping lookout, and this fits well with a fable about the bird.

James Lipton directs us to the 1885 book *The Folklore and Provincial Names of British Birds*, in which the Reverend Charles Swainson gives his version of the story of the nightingale and the blindworm, each of whom had only one eye. Legend has it that having been invited to the wedding of the wren, the nightingale felt so ashamed of having only one eye that it stole the single eye of the blindworm, leaving it with none. But the worm swore it would steal back its eye under cover of darkness while the nightingale slept, so the bird vowed never to sleep at night and instead to keep a nocturnal watch, singing its distinctive song all night through.

A PARLIAMENT
OF OWLS

This group name appears in many modern lists of collective nouns, but none of the medieval lists, or indeed the eighteenth-century ones, include any term for a gathering of owls. It seems instead to have its origins in the 1950s children's classic *The Chronicles of Narnia*, in which C. S. Lewis makes several subtle references to medieval literature. The work we're concerned with here is Chaucer's allegorical poem 'The Parliament of Fowls', in which all the birds of the earth gather together to find a mate. Lewis adapts the title of Chaucer's poem to describe a council of owls who meet at night to discuss the affairs of Narnia, and uses it as a chapter heading in *The Silver Chair*, the sixth book in the series.

The huge international success of the books – they've sold over 100 million copies and are published in forty-seven languages – means that the term has become far more widely known than most of the traditional collective nouns and is now recognized by dictionary compliers as the 'correct' term for a group of owls. In fact, 'a parliament' is used in the fifteenth-century lists as a group name for rooks, not owls (see 'a building or a parliament of rooks').

A COVEY OF PARTRIDGES OR GROUSE

Hunting grouse and partridge was such a popular pastime in medieval England that the natural environment was changed to make for the best possible hunting conditions. This often included burning the heather that grew naturally on the heathland and managing the growth of shrubs and bushes to create the bird's preferred nesting environment. Both birds were considered delicious to eat and were regularly served at the tables of the nobility.

The word 'covey' appeared as a collective noun to describe them in *The Book of St Albans* and several other fifteenth-century lists and the term is still used by huntsmen and women today. Unlike coots, whose group name 'a covert' seems incongruous when compared to the bird's ostentatious behaviour, partridges and grouse do make some attempt to conceal their nests and themselves from predators by surrounding their nests with twigs and brambles. Pliny the Elder in his *Natural History* describes behaviour in the adult bird that could also justify the noun:

If a fowler approaches the nest, the hen will lure
him away by running away while pretending to be
injured. If the hen has no eggs to protect, she does not
run but lies on her back in a furrow and holds a clod
of earth in her claws to cover herself.

In fact, though, covey comes from the Latin *cubare*, a
root it shares with the word 'incubate'. Just as in the
case of the coot, the term refers to the newly hatched
chicks rather than to the adult birds.

A MUSTER OF PEACOCKS

American author Washington Irving refers to
the accepted use of this noun in his short story
'Christmas Day', which appears in his 1819–20 work
The Sketch Book of Geoffrey Crayon, Gent:

There appeared to be an unusual number of peacocks
about the place, and I was making some remarks
upon what I termed a flock of them, that were
basking under a sunny wall, when I was gently
corrected in my phraseology by Master Simon,
who told me that, according to the most ancient

and approved treatise on hunting, I must say a
MUSTER of peacocks.

Sadly for us, Master Simon provides no elucidation on the matter of why 'muster' was chosen as the proper phrase by the author of that ancient and approved treatise, but clearly it was important that a gentleman should get it right. The term probably comes from the French word *moustre*, meaning show or view, a reference to the male peacock's mating season ritual of parading its impressive tail to attract a likely peahen. In the Egerton Manuscript, muster is printed 'monster', and in the Porkington Manuscript it's 'mostur', both of which can be translated as muster. The word is also a military term for a formal gathering of troops, which applies especially to gatherings for a display, so perhaps displays of feathers and of soldiers have the same source.

A NYE OF PHEASANT

There's an interesting passage about this company term in Sir Arthur Conan Doyle's historical novel *Sir Nigel*, in which the young gentleman is educated in the language of the hunt by the Knight of Duplin, head huntsman of the King. The knight mocks a young lord who made the mistake of describing a flock of pheasants as a covey:

'How would you have said it, Nigel?'
'Surely, fair sir, it should be a nye of pheasants.
'Good Nigel – a nye of pheasants, even as it is a
gaggle of geese, a badling of ducks, a fall of woodcock
or a wisp of snipe. But a covey of pheasants! What
sort of talk is that?'

But the 'correct' traditional term isn't quite as categorically clear as the knight suggests. The medieval manuscripts offer several different spellings of the word; *The Book of St Albans* has 'a nye', the Egerton Manuscript has 'a ny', one manuscript in the Harley collection has 'a ye' and another says, 'Ye shall say I haue fonde a couey of pertirch a beuy of Quayles and eye of fesauntes.'

James Lipton found a discussion of the term

in *The Illustrated Sporting and Dramatic News* while researching *An Exaltation of Larks,* which asserted that the correct term should be 'an eye', which is the Old English word for a brood. All authorities agree that all spellings and versions apply only to the young, which does suggest that the knight may have been just slightly mistaken.

A CONGREGATION OF PLOVERS

In the medieval lists the word 'congregation' is used to describe groups of people and of plovers. Despite its seeming suitability for any gathering of birds or creatures, it's only these two for whom the term was codified as a 'proper' collective noun. None of the explorations into the history of these terms that preceded this one have shed any light on why this might be, and yet the term has endured. When the descriptively titled *Field Book or Sports and Pastimes of the United Kingdom Compiled from Sources Ancient and Modern* was printed in 1833 its author offered a neat explanation for this and several other company names: 'There was a peculiar kind of language invented by sportsmen of the Middle Ages, which it was necessary for them to be acquainted with, and some of the terms are still continued.' And there you have it.

AN UNKINDNESS
OF RAVENS

The Devil had a lot to answer for in the popular culture of the Middle Ages. Times were hard, failed harvests and virulent disease meant that death often came too soon and with only a poor understanding of the true causes of such calamities, it's not hard to see why the Devil was so often held responsible.

In this climate, anything associated with death was seen as evil and ominous. As carrion birds, ravens often circled when an animal was close to its end. This behaviour, combined with their black feathers, gave them a sinister reputation. Literary references, such as these famous lines from Shakespeare's *Macbeth*, have helped cement this notion:

> *The Raven himself is hoarse*
> *That croaks the fatal entrance of Duncan*
> *Under my battlements.*

But the birds' own habits are as much to blame for the public perception of their unkindness. Hodgkin's analysis of *The Book of St Albans* points us to *The Folklore and Provincial Names of British Birds* by Charles Swainson (1885), which explains: 'Ancient writers held the opinion that the raven was utterly wanting in parental care, expelling its young ones from the nest, leaving them prematurely to shift for themselves.'

Swainson also noted the ancient observer's view that this unkindness was repaid by the raven's young, quoting from English doctor John Swan's *Speculum Mundi* of 1635, which says: '[When] they be old, and have their bills overgrown, they die of famine . . . Neither will their young ones help them, but rather set upon them when they are not able to resist.'

A BUILDING OR A PARLIAMENT OF ROOKS

Appearing on many of the medieval lists, 'a building of rooks' takes its inspiration from the huge rookeries the birds nest in each spring. John Hodgkin writes that the term likely stems from the fact that rooks 'make such a fuss' over the building of their nests. Female rooks are known to fight noisily over nest-building materials, mostly breaking twigs and branches from the tops of trees or stealing them from other birds' nests rather than searching for broken ones. At their largest, rookeries can be home to a thousand birds and their chicks, who are fully fledged after a month in the nest.

The intensive construction work carried out by

the bird is described in children's poem 'The Rooks', written in 1876 by Jane Euphemia Browne:

The rooks are building on the trees;
They build there every spring:
'Caw, caw,' is all they say,
For none of them can sing.

They're up before the break of day,
And up till late at night;
For they must labour busily
As long as it is light.

And many a crooked stick they bring,
And many a slender twig,
And many a tuft of moss, until
Their nests are round and big.

The final verse puts perfectly the reason large flocks of rook are also sometimes known as 'a parliament':

'Caw, caw!' Oh, what a noise
They make in rainy weather!
Good children always speak by turns,
But rooks all talk together.

A DOPPING OF SHELDRAKE

John Hodgkin comes to our aid again here with his extensive linguistic detective work and offers a definition for dopping that he found in use in East Anglia to describe 'a short quick curtsey', which he feels perfectly describes the way sheldrake suddenly dip down beneath the surface of the water when they sense danger.

Several late medieval documents describe 'dopping worship', a bowing, bobbing kind of praying that was condemned as popish during the Reformation. The sixteenth-century play *The Return from Parnassus Part 1*, the author of which is unknown, uses the word in context in lines delivered by the stage keeper:

That scraping leg, that dopping courtesy,
That fawning bow,
those sycophant's smooth terms
Gained our stage much favour, did they not?

In fact, the distinctive bobbing of the sheldrake beneath the surface of the water is usually for feeding rather than for coverage. Sheldrake, now more commonly referred to as shelducks, eat vegetation, aquatic snails and insects floating beneath them and duck their heads under water every time they're ready for a snack.

A HOST OF SPARROWS

John Hodgkin is unusually accepting of this group name calling 'an ost of sparrowis' – as it features in *The Book of St Albans* – a true company term and adding, 'There is the notion of an army or hostile force, and not without cause, from their destructive habits.'

Host comes from the Latin word *hostis*, meaning stranger or enemy, and in medieval Latin it described an army. English translations of the Bible that followed this used the word to mean an army of God: we're familiar with a host of angels, and the heavenly host. Sparrows certainly have a reputation for aggression, often leaving a path of destruction in their wake. They tear down the nests of swallows and house martins, strip new leaves from trees and excavate any possible nesting sites, which often include nooks and crannies in manmade buildings. Their ability to adapt their diet to whatever food they can most readily find means that they can also be responsible for the depletion of grain stores and the decimation of fruit crops. This is still troublesome nowadays but could have been disastrous for the medieval farmer whose livelihood depended on the tiny margin of profit he could make from each harvest.

In 1970 James Lipton offered 'a ubiquity of sparrows', though in light of the sadly dwindling numbers these days, 'a scarcity of sparrows' might be more apt.

A MURMURATION OF STARLINGS

The Egerton Manuscript listed a 'murmuracyon' back in 1468 and most subsequent lists from the fifteenth century include this entry. As with many terms describing flocks of birds this one is inspired by the sound the birds make when they're flocking together.

Starlings are gregarious birds and spend most months of the year in large flocks. They have an incredible range of vocal tools, chattering, chuckling, imitating other birds and even copying non-bird sounds, like tractor engines or motorbikes. In recent years their numbers have been declining but huge flocks of the birds can still be seen swooping and wheeling together in the skies when they prepare for roosting. The birds have been studied closely to help ornithologists to understand flocking behaviour and we now know that though the flock looks as though its movement is co-ordinated en masse, it is in fact governed by each bird's reactions to the few birds that are its immediate neighbours in the flock, so it maintains its distance from them and flies in the same direction as the majority. Starlings exhibit this awe-inspiring pattern when they're looking for a suitable roost for the whole flock to spend the night, so it's best observed at dusk over woodland in the autumn, when it's possible in some parts of the UK to see up to 100,000 birds in a single murmuration.

A FLIGHT OF SWALLOWS

Swallows had been revered since the days of the earliest civilizations when they were believed to be sacred to the Penates, or house gods of the ancient Romans. The fact that the birds seemed always to be in flight meant that they were seen as spiritual creatures, at home in the heavens, and their agility on the wing meant their aerial displays were watched, as they still are today, with awe.

Because people rarely saw the birds land there was also a belief among the medieval peasantry that swallows had no feet, thus early creators of collective nouns chose 'a flight' for a group of swallows. In the Middle Ages people used signals from the natural world to predict sunshine or showers and while the first sighting of a swallow was said to herald the arrival of summer, a low-flying bird was read as a sign that rain was on the way. Robert Louis Stevenson's poem 'Swallows Travel To and Fro' also links the bird with the weather:

Swallows travel to and fro,
And the great winds come and go,
And the steady breezes blow,
Bearing perfume, bearing love.
Breezes hasten, swallows fly,
Towered clouds forever ply,
And at noonday, you and I
See the same sunshine above.

◆　◆　◆

A GAME OF SWANS

The Book of St Albans offers the predictable 'herde of swannys', the same group name used for the revered deer in recognition of the bird's regal status (see also 'a herd of wrens'). But there is another term for them that sheds light on their fascinating history. In the records of Romsey Abbey lies the 1554 will of William Romsey of Bieton, in which he writes: 'My game of swannes to remain to Elizabeth my wyffe during her lyffe and at her decease at the marking time next after to remain to Anne Bartilmew and Kunegunde Dix and the heirs of their bodies lawfully begotten.' Their inclusion in medieval wills and testaments reveals the special status of the bird; swans had been decreed a 'royal bird', which meant that no individual could claim ownership of a swan without the permission of the crown. In bestowing this privilege the crown granted a 'swan mark', a particular way of marking the birds' beaks – in the days before tagging and micro-chipping – to show who they belonged to.

Under Elizabeth I over 900 individuals and corporations had a game of swans with their own unique mark. Ancient documents describe the process of 'swan-upping', annual expeditions to the rivers and lakes swans used for breeding, to mark the beaks of the newly hatched young birds. Over time 'game' came to be used to describe any flock of swans, as James Joyce shows in *A Portrait of the Artist as a Young Man*: 'The park trees were heavy with rain; and rain fell still and ever in the lake, lying grey like a shield. A game of swans flew there and the water and the shore beneath were fouled with their green-white slime.'

A MUTATION OF THRUSHES

This strange-sounding company term offers a fascinating insight into medieval misconceptions about the natural world. The study of nature, including the physiology and behaviour of birds and animals, dates back to the ancient Roman and Greek empires, but sometimes there were gaps in scientific knowledge that were filled with beliefs that seem incredibly unlikely today. In his interpretation of medieval company terms Hodgkin includes a fascinating letter written by a Mr William Dodgson to the editor of Harwicke's *Science Gossip* (published in the later 1800s), in which he states: 'It is a recognized fact amongst naturalists that thrushes acquire new legs, and cast the old ones when about ten years old.' Whether this theory truly held sway amongst fifteenth-century naturalists is hard to test, but it would certainly explain the unusual group name.

Thrushes, like many birds, do undergo a physical change of sorts when they moult and grow new, thicker feathers for the winter months, and this has also been described historically as a 'mutation'. Thomas Hardy, in his poem 'The Darkling Thrush', describes the hope-inspiring power of the thrush's song in winter:

> *At once a voice arose among*
> *The bleak twigs overhead*
> *In a full-hearted evensong*
> *Of joy illimited;*
> *An aged thrush, frail, gaunt, and small,*
> *In blast-beruffled plume,*
> *Had chosen thus to fling his soul*
> *Upon the growing gloom.*

A PITYING OF TURTLE DOVES

The turtle dove is also known as the mourning dove because of the tragic timbre of its call. If you can't immediately call to mind its song, it's the plaintive coo you often hear on a summer's evening that sounds like this: 'woo WOO woo, woo-woo'. An elderly relative of mine once told me she'd been taught to recognize the song by hearing in it the sorrowful refrain 'my HEART bleeds, Betty', a sentiment that fits the tone perfectly. Scottish-born American ornithologist Alexander Wilson, who produced a popular guide to local bird life in 1840, described the call as sounding 'as if the afflicted creature were just recovering its voice from the last convulsive sobs of distress'.

Poets through the ages have used turtle doves as a representation of sorrow. In his 1828 epic poem *Eccelino da Romano, Surnamed the Tyrant of Padua*, Irish peer and writer Henry Augustus Dillon Lee included the lines:

> *Piteous as turtle-dove, that from the nest*
> *Beholds her mate torn by the cruel hawk.*

Indeed 'a piteousness' of turtle doves is interchangeable with 'a pitying', though the latter is the first to appear in print, in the fifteenth-century Porkington Manuscript of Middle English miscellany. Before then, 'a dule of doves' was the accepted collective noun and it is this term that appears in the fourteenth-century *The Book of St Albans*. In those days, 'dole' meant sorrow or grief and came via Old French from the Latin *dolēre*, to feel pain or to grieve. Two further lists have a more uplifting offering, however: 'a truelove of turtle doves', inspired by the birds' lifetime devotion to a single mate.

A PLUMP OF
WILDFOWL

Wildfowl can refer to any game bird, duck, goose or quail, all of which were regularly found on the banqueting tables of the medieval nobility. Records of a feast held in honour of King Richard II and John of Gaunt, the Duke of Lancaster in 1387 offer a fascinating insight into the ostentatiousness of celebratory dining in the Middle Ages. The list of foods includes: 12 salted and 2 fresh oxen, 120 sheep heads, 12 boar, 14 calves, 140 pigs, 1,200 pigeons, 10 dozen curlews and 'wild fowle ynogh' – which translates simply as 'enough wildfowl'.

The plumpness of the wildfowl was probably what made them so popular to eat, but according to the *OED* by the fifteenth century 'a plump' was being used to describe 'a group of people, animals, or things; troop; cluster'.

Hunting for wildfowl was a popular pastime and many of the medieval hunting handbooks are packed with details of how to hone skills at the 'sport'. Though practised illegally by the peasantry it was deemed a pursuit worthy of royalty with a long and illustrious history dating back to at least the tenth century, when King Heinrich of Germany was given the epithet 'the fowler' because he was said to have received his call to the throne while he was out repairing his birding nets.

A FALL OF WOODCOCK

Woodcock were a popular quarry of the medieval hunt and they were often served roasted at the tables of the aristocracy. About the size of a quail, the birds are sturdy and squat and stay close to the ground, so hunters would need to flush them into the open with dogs or by beating the bushes they hid in. Noblemen used hawks to catch the birds but historian Richard Almond explains in his book *Medieval Hunting* that the woodcock habitually breaks cover from its day roost in the evening and takes the same flight path to feed, so commoners would erect large nets attached to long wooden poles between two trees to snare them in. Almond also reports on another method of catching woodcock, depicted in a fourteenth-century illumination in *The Book of the Hunt of King Modus*, written in France by hunting expert Henri de Ferrières. For this technique, a member of the hunt is shown dressed up as a woodcock, including a long nose-piece for a beak, waddling up to slip a horsehair noose around the bird's neck.

The collective noun 'a fall' seems to come from observations of the way large numbers of the birds would suddenly appear in the bushes overnight, after a change in wind direction. The birds are migratory and large numbers would appear on the British coast in autumn. The first full moon in November is sometimes described as the 'woodcock moon' because it marks the time of their sudden arrival. Researchers suggest that 'a fall of woodcock' is used in the same way that we might use the term 'a fall of snow' to describe a sudden covering of snow.

A DESCENT OF WOODPECKERS

This first appeared in the list of collective nouns found at the end of fifteenth-century monk John Lydgate's poem 'A Disputation between a Horse, a Sheepe and a Goose, for Superioritie', printed by William Caxton in 1476. Unusually, despite the fact that all these lists were shaped by previous lists and were copied by subsequent compilers, this one wasn't included in any other medieval collections of group names.

There are three possible sources of inspiration, all of which come from observations of the bird's behaviour. Though woodpeckers spend most of their time in trees, using the repetitive pecking of their beaks against the bark of trees to draw out the insects they feed on, they also search for their preferred meal of ants on the woodland floor. To catch them the woodpecker drops down from the tree to the ground to feed. A second reason for its descent is the bird's characteristic pattern of moving from tree to tree by swooping from high in the branches of one tree down to the base of the next, ready to begin its drumming again. A third possibility is the movement of the woodpecker from the top of the trunk down to the roots as it grips the bark with its talons and moves steadily downwards, pecking at a rate of twenty impacts per minute and feeding as it goes.

A HERD OF WRENS

The Book of St Albans has 'an herde of wrennys' and John Hodgkin says: 'The wren was probably allowed the term of "herd" – the word applied to harts – because it was the king of birds.' The hart was the stag of the red deer, the most prized of all royal hunting quarry, and Hodgkin's reference to the wren being king of the birds comes from an ancient fable, known to both Aristotle and Pliny and revived in the Middle Ages as a popular folktale.

It tells the story of how all the birds gathered together to settle disputes between them by electing a king. They each showed off their skills, and the wren was praised for being able to hatch twelve chicks in one nest, but it was decided that the bird who could fly the highest should be crowned king. They all soared skyward and the eagle flew high above them all and cried out 'I am king!' But as he spoke the tiny wren emerged from the feathers under his wing and fluttered up above his head to claim the crown. The two birds spiralled down to earth together and all the birds agreed that the clever wren should be their king.

The tale inspired a children's song traditional in Ireland and on the Isle of Man that begins:

> *The Wren, the Wren the king of all birds,*
> *St. Stephenses day,*
> *he was caught in the furze.*
> *Although he is little, his honor is great,*
> *Rise up, kind sir, and give us a trate.*

CHAPTER 7

EXOTIC
CREATURES

A SHREWDNESS OF APES

At first glance, it's hard to believe that this particular collective noun was in use a full 500 years ago. To us, shrewdness means intelligence and more precisely, astuteness. It describes a considered kind of cleverness that implies an ability to make careful judgements and act accordingly. And though recent studies into the behaviour and brains of apes have revealed startling cognitive abilities, these findings would have shocked medieval naturalists, who lacked the means to make such detailed observations of the creatures in their natural habitat. Instead, our fifteenth-century forefathers noted in apes a kind of playful mischievousness, and a closer look at the way the word shrewdness was used when it was included in *The Book of St Albans* reveals that it was in fact the perfect word to convey this.

In the prologue to 'The Wife of Bath's Tale' from Chaucer's *Canterbury Tales* we can see the word used in its medieval context:

> *Of Phasiphae, that was queen of Crete,*
> *For shrewedness he thought the tale sweet.*

Translations reveal that the word means wickedness. It came from *shrew*, meaning dogged or wicked and also from *shrewen*, to curse.

In a wonderful stroke of luck the evolution of our language has mirrored the evolution of our scientific understanding, so that a term that made perfect sense to Dame Juliana Barnes in 1486 can also make perfect sense to us, despite the fact that the meaning of the word and our view of the animal it describes have undergone five centuries of change.

A TROOP OF BABOONS

This is one of the more well-established collective nouns that is very much in regular use. It doesn't appear in *The Book of St Albans* but is listed in Joseph Strutt's *Sports and Pastimes of the People of England*, printed in 1801, and the fact that it is still employed today owes much to the fact that zoologists have regular opportunity to use it.

While many collective terms are rendered unusable in everyday life because of the solitary nature of the creatures they describe, the highly sociable habits of the baboon mean that this one has real applications. Most baboons live in groups of between fifty and two hundred animals and understanding the dynamics of these large, hierarchical societies is central to the study of the species. Shared baby-rearing and hours of grooming cement relationships between the females of the troop while displays of physical strength determine the pecking order among the males, who usually leave their birth group before they reach the age of sexual maturity and work their way into a new troop.

Violent tussles have been observed between rival troops, and it's easy to imagine that the collective noun has military links. But though the word troop was used to describe a group of soldiers, and more specifically a subdivision of a cavalry force from the 1580s onwards, the word originally came from the Old French *trope*, which simply meant a band or company of people.

◆ ◆ ◆

A SLOTH OF BEARS

Appearing in *The Book of St Albans* as 'a slowth' of bears, this noun is a reference to the slow ambling pace of the bear as it makes its way along woodland pathways, though they were anything but slow when under attack. Hunting for bears, especially on the Iberian Peninsula, was popular because of the animal's stamina and strength, and the danger of the hunt. In his examination of the *St Albans* list John Hodgkin uses this fact to back up his view that many terms of assembly were not intended as nouns at all, and that the lists of terms were in fact simply the proper descriptive words to use in a discussion of an animal's behaviour or movements.

In England 'a slowth' of bears would rarely have been used in practice because bears were baited, rather than hunted. During the 1500s this form of entertainment was so popular that 'bear gardens' were built with circular areas surrounded by high fencing and raised seating so spectators could watch chained bears attempting to defend themselves against hunting dogs. Henry VIII had a bear garden built at Whitehall and Elizabeth I was such a fan of the spectacle that she overrode an attempt by Parliament to ban the sport from being carried out on Sundays. It remained a popular pastime until the nineteenth century.

AN OBSTINACY OF BUFFALO

This is a prime example of the kind of collective noun that takes inspiration from the characteristics of the animal it describes. Buffalo are herd animals living primarily in the plains and forests of Africa and South-East Asia. Their powerful herding instincts protect them from predators like lions, wolves and bears, which usually target the weakest members of the group. When one animal sees or hears something it perceives as a threat, it begins to run headlong away from the danger. Instantly and instinctively the other animals follow suit, jamming their bodies against each other as they go to prevent their predator from penetrating their ranks. This densely packed, high-speed storm of hides and hooves is what is known as a stampede. Once a stampede has begun, there is no stopping or diverting it. Plains Indians who have hunted buffalo for around 2,000 years made use of this fact by triggering a stampede near the edge of a sheer cliff, knowing that the buffalo would run straight off the edge and that many would die in the fall. It's easy to see how they came to be seen as obstinate. But their stubbornness isn't always born from blind panic or the unswerving urge to follow the pack. Sometimes after an animal is wounded by a hunter or predator, the herd will double back on themselves and ambush their attackers.

A BASK OF CROCODILES

Basking is crucial to crocodiles. They're not just resting when you see them sitting on a rock, they're actually busy regulating their body temperature. A massive advantage of being cold-blooded or, to use the proper term (as Dame Juliana would surely have wished) – ectothermic, is the ability to go for long periods of time without food. Much of the food eaten by warm-blooded animals like us is converted by the body into heat, but this means that our bodies require constant re-fuelling. Large crocodiles can go for an entire year without food if they need to, living on the energy stored in their bodies.

The big evolutionary trade-off, of course, is that reptiles cannot generate heat without exposing their bodies to sunlight. And this is where basking comes in. Usually around mid-morning, when the angle of the sun's rays is optimal, crocodiles find a sunny spot on a rock or even on a broad branch of a tree, haul themselves out of the water, and lie still, allowing the external source of heat to raise their core body temperature. If they feel themselves getting a little too hot they open their mouths slightly, which serves the same purpose as panting for a dog, until they've raised their temperatures enough to help them with digestion and hunting. During this period of basking, crocodiles are often highly social, congregating at the best basking sites and sometimes also hunting and rearing young together.

A HERD OF ELEPHANTS

For most medieval Europeans, the likelihood of coming across a group of elephants was slim. In the luxuriantly illustrated bestiaries of the time they are often depicted as super-sized oxen with long noses and downward- or upward-pointing tusks, a reminder of how strange it must have been to hear descriptions of these unlikely sounding creatures.

Elephants were grouped together in the public imagination with other fantastical-sounding beasts that in fact turned out to be mythological. They were said to be the sworn enemy of dragons, who were believed to use elephant blood to cool their fiery stomachs, and were often shown in medieval art doing battle with either dragons or unicorns. A true-to-life representation of an elephant dating from between 1275 and 1300 can be seen in a carving on the underside of a folding seat in Exeter Cathedral, by which time elephants had arrived in western Europe as gifts for the royal menageries. A fascinating insight into their mysterious reputation can be found in the Harley Manuscript, dated around 1260:

They are possessed of a vigorous intelligence and memory. They move about in herds (they salute with such movements as they are capable of), are afraid of a mouse, and are disinclined to breed. They bring forth after two years [gestation], and they do not produce young more than once, and then not several but only one. They live 300 years.

Later compilers of collective nouns have listed alternatives to the generic 'herd' and suggest instead 'a parade' or 'a memory'.

A GANG OF ELK

The elk was believed to be the same as the red deer, with which it shares many physical characteristics. Elk are described in *The Book of St Albans* but no group name is given to them in the list. They are named in Joseph Strutt's *Sports and Pastimes of the People of England* as one of the 'beasts of sweet flight' to be found in medieval hunting manuals.

However, recent DNA testing has shown clear genetic differences between the two types of deer, and in fact elk was never hunted in medieval England because it has been extinct on the British Isles since around 1500 BC. In Scandinavia, though, it continued to flourish, and in North America it was also widely hunted. In fact, 'a gang of elk' first appears in print in American essayist Washington Irving's history of John Astor's fur trading colony, *Astoria*, published in 1836, in which he writes: 'Besides the buffaloes they saw an abundance of deer, and frequent gangs of stately elks, together with light troops of sprightly antelopes, the fleetest and most beautiful inhabitants of the prairies.'

'Gang' appears to have had none of the negative connotations that it has today; the word comes from the Old Norse *ganga*, linked to our words gait and going. The *OED* explains its original meaning as 'going, a journey', which in Middle English became 'a way' and also 'a set of things or people which go together'. The term could have evolved as a specific description for the smaller groups of young male elk who roam a range of 600 square miles as they mature before the breeding season.

A BAND OF GORILLAS

This noun didn't feature in the medieval lists because back then, no one knew that gorillas existed. There had been one possible sighting of the animal by ancient Greek explorer Hanno, who in the fifth century BC described having seen 'an island filled

with savage people, most of them women, and covered in hair. Our interpreters call them gorillae.'
It was from this description that the animals get their name. But medieval Europeans had no access to this Ancient Greek intelligence and it wasn't until 1625 that another account of the animals was made by English explorer Andrew Batell. Even then there was still no proof of the creature's existence and it was 1847 before western physician Thomas Savage wrote the first recognized account of the species and backed up his findings with bones and a skull he had found in Liberia.

The noun is one of the few describing animals that is officially used today, and it may have its roots in the study of human beings. In anthropology, a small sub-group of a tribe of indigenous people is referred to as a band, and since the first explorers to come across gorillas believed them to be primitive people, it makes sense that they might refer to a group of them in the same way.

Some modern lists of company terms give 'a whoop of gorillas', which comes from 1970s UK comedy show *Not the Nine O'Clock News*. Rowan Atkinson appears as a cultured and articulate gorilla named Gerald, who informs his interviewer of the correct collective noun for his species as well as the fact that a group of baboons is known as a flange.

A BLOAT OF HIPPOPOTAMI

This is a comparatively recent addition to the collective noun canon, appearing for the first time in print in C. E. Hare's 1939 hunting and fishing manual *The Language of Field Sports*. The main body of Hare's book was derived from older sources and his list of company terms sticks to the medieval tradition of copying from previous publications. But, like compilers before and after him, Hare couldn't resist making up a few of his own. This one has stuck, perhaps because it so perfectly conjures an image of the creature.

Hippos are the third largest land animal – only elephants and white rhinos are bigger – and an average male weighs just under 8,000 pounds. Their bodies are covered in a layer of subcutaneous fat that helps them to float well in the rivers that make their homes and they move laboriously on land, where they graze for up to four hours a night. It's likely that they genuinely do spend much of their time with bloated stomachs since their diet is almost exclusively grass and they often store what they've ingested. They can go for up to three weeks without eating.

Another modern name for a herd of hippos is 'a pod', which is interesting in light of a recent study of the animal's DNA, which revealed that though their name means 'river horse' in Ancient Greek, they are in fact much more closely related to dolphins – who are also often referred to as a pod.

A LEAP OF LEOPARDS

Most medieval Europeans hadn't seen exotic animals in the flesh. There were collections of animals kept by European royalty, and Crusaders travelling to the Holy Lands may have seen menageries in Constantinople and Cyprus, but the general populace relied instead on images in heraldic and church art and on accounts of exotic beasts in fables and biblical tales. As a result, the occasional misapprehension crept in. In the Middle Ages, leopards were thought to be a crossbreed between a lion and a mythical spotted beast, illustrated in medieval bestiaries, called a pard. Their name was a blend of the two ('leo' from lion). Thirteenth-century scholar Bartholomaeus Anglicus gives his understanding of the animal as:

The leopard is a beast most cruel, and is gendered in spouse-breach of a pard and of a lioness, and pursueth his prey startling and leaping and not running, and if he taketh not his prey in the third leap, or in the fourth, then he stinteth for indignation, and goeth backward as though he were overcome.

So while the leopard's origins remained obscure to the medieval observer, its technique of springing onto its prey was well known, and a 'leap of leopards' had a pleasing alliterative quality that must have appealed to the poetically minded originators of proper company terms. It appeared from the Egerton Manuscript onwards as 'a lepe of lybardys' and was translated into modern English in several of the seventeenth- and eighteenth-century collections, but it hasn't had the staying power of 'a pride of lions', possibly because leopards are so resolutely solitary.

A PRIDE OF LIONS

This group name is one of the oldest, appearing in the French manuscripts that the English lists used as source material, and yet it is one of the few that is still widely used today. While all other big cats are solitary hunters, lions live in social groups of around ten animals and often hunt as a pack, so perhaps its durability owes something to the fact that the term could be put to use.

Sir Arthur Conan Doyle's historical novel *Sir Nigel* sheds light on the importance of all collective nouns to the hunt, but especially this one. In one scene, the young eponymous knight is taught by the King's head huntsman, who quizzes his charge on how he would describe different groups of animals:

'And if they be lions? . . .'
'Surely, fair sir, I would be content to say that I had seen a number of lions, if indeed I could say aught after so wondrous an adventure.'
'Nay, Nigel, a huntsman would have said that he had seen a pride of lions, and so proved that he knew the language of the chase.'

Pride probably came to the minds of the originators of venereal terms because of the animals' place at the top of the food chain in the jungle. Apart from humans, lions have no predators and have long been described as noble because of their position at the head of the animal kingdom's hierarchy. Pride at this time meant a proper sense of pride in one's own high standing, rather than the kind of pride that comes before a fall in the modern age.

A TROOP OR BARREL OF MONKEYS

A troop of monkeys is the older of the terms used to describe these intelligent primates, who get their group noun from the way they form tightly knit social groups with a clearly defined leader in the form of an alpha male. They also show aggression to neighbouring troops, just as troops of cavalry might. In fact, some species exhibit displays of strength along the borders of their territories in just the way hostile troops of soldiers do. Gibbons, howler monkeys and siamangs are all capable of loud vocalisations to aid them in this ritualistic form of intimidation, designed to warn 'enemy' troops off from encroaching on their food supplies.

In fact, before the word troop was used to describe fighting forces, it was used to mean a group of people or things, stemming from the medieval Latin word *troppus*, meaning flock. There are several alternative names for a group of monkeys; Shakespeare gives us 'a wilderness of monkeys' to signify a huge number of them in *The Merchant of Venice*:

> *Tubal: One of them showed me a ring that he had of your daughter for a monkey.*
> *Shylock: Out upon her! Thou torturest me, Tubal. It was my turquoise. I had it of Leah when I was a bachelor. I would not have given it for a wilderness of monkeys.*

And the phrase 'more fun than a barrel of monkeys' has been in use since the nineteenth century. The *OED* has a similar version in print for the first time in 1840 in G. Darley's chronicle of Thomas à Becket: 'De Traci chatters more than a cage of monkeys: we must wait.'

A TURMOIL OF PORPOISES

Like many terms describing types of dolphin and whale, this noun was popularized by its use by whalers during the sixteenth century. While porpoises in a group are more commonly called 'a pod', this term has the advantage of conveying an image of the water

in which a pod of porpoises might meet.

Porpoises are the fastest swimmers of any creature in the sea and they also dive and leap, making the water seem to boil when groups of them congregate. Like dolphins, porpoises are intelligent and sociable, often gathering in groups of up to twenty and sometimes swimming nose to nose and fin to fin. They also interact with humans and will often follow a ship and swim alongside it. It's easy to imagine how a hardy whaler, at sea for up to four years at a time, might have looked down to the black water beside his ship, choppy and bubbling with the dancing bodies of a porpoise pod, and decided that the only way to accurately describe the scene was as 'a turmoil'.

A CRASH OF
RHINOCEROS

Thanks to the popularity of African safaris, this collective noun has developed a gravitas appropriate for the description of a herd of these enormous beasts and is widely used in the records of animal sightings at game reserves. The term takes its inspiration from the behaviour of the male animals during the mating season, when rival rhinos charge each other when competing for a female. Male rhinos can charge at up to 30 miles per hour and with two tonnes of weight each the impact can be huge.

The rhino's horn is rarely used to inflict injury on opponents, though. The horns are made from matted hair that grows throughout the animal's life. The decimation of the rhino population by poachers is largely due to the belief, particularly prevalent in South-East Asia, that their horns have healing properties.

The strangeness of the animals' appearance made rhinos popular in the European menageries of exotic animals kept by the royalty of the fifteenth and sixteenth centuries. In 1515 Portuguese King Manuel I arranged for a fight between a rhinoceros and an elephant to test a legend that the beasts were mortal enemies. In medieval bestiaries they are usually depicted doing battle with elephants, and are often interchangeable with unicorns in accounts from the

Middle Ages. King Manuel's courtyard was the scene of this test and when the curtain that separated the beasts was drawn back the rhino charged, causing the young elephant to flee and cementing the myth of the animals' animosity.

A BALE OF TURTLES

This is a delightful example of the kind of fifteenth-century-style Chinese whispers that characterizes so many of the traditional lists of collective nouns. C. E. Hare's attempt to get to the bottom of the mysterious term ended with a presumption that it must have been a misunderstanding on the part of the scribes, since turtle doves were often referred to simply as turtles, and a flock of turtle doves were described in some early lists as 'a dule'. This came from the French *deuil*, meaning mourning, in reference to the birds' plaintive song. His suggestion is that the scribe miscopied dule as bale and so a new collective noun was created.

There is certainly no obvious link between turtles and the word bale, which is usually used to describe a bundle of hay, though its etymology might hold a clue. It was first used in Middle English having come via Middle Dutch from Old French. The *OED* explains that it is ultimately of Germanic origin and that it's related to the word ball. It may be stretching the bounds of possibility to suggest a true link here but for supposition's sake, turtle's eggs, which they lay in their hundreds in nests at their natal breeding grounds, do look like little white golf balls, and since many collective nouns describing animals, birds and sea life are inspired by the young or the nest, it feels possible, if not probable, that this could have been the source. At least, that's probably what that poor mistaken fifteenth-century scribe would like us to think.

◆　◆　◆

A GAM OF WHALES

A gam is defined by the *OED* as 'a herd or school of whales; also whaling ships in company' and was used to describe a social gathering of whalers at sea – a welcome occasion of companionship in what could otherwise be lonely voyages, with several years being spent at sea. When two whaling ships sailed past each other, the captains would steer the vessels side by side and the crew from one ship would ferry across to the other. It was a chance to socialize, share news, exchange information about good hunting grounds and break the tedium of life on the ocean. Some ships even had a 'gamming chair' – a large wooden armchair on ropes that could be hung on a spar between the two ships and used to swing the women and children from one ship to the other.

As whalers used this term to denote a get-together, it seems natural that they should use it to describe gatherings of their prey. In fact, it's impossible to know whether the term was first used to describe groups of whales or whalers. Whales are certainly often seen collectively. They're highly intelligent mammals and have strong social ties; some species of whale hunt in groups, share the care of their calves and make their migratory journeys together. In the open ocean they can sometimes be observed at the surface diving and gliding past each other. The word gam is thought to stem from 'game', which seems apt for either get-together.

A ZEAL OF ZEBRA

This doesn't appear in any early collections, or even in James Lipton's *An Exaltation of Larks*, which includes over a thousand real and fanciful group terms, so it seems likely that it's one of the most recent additions to the list of company names.

It is mentioned in *The Origins of English Words: A Discursive Dictionary of Indo–European Roots* by etymologist Joseph Twadell Shipley, published in 1984, but only as an example of the way some collective nouns are simply amusing inventions. Finding no distinguishable roots for the phrase he surmises that this one has 'been created by word fanciers seeking clever or humorous pairings'.

Certainly the double 'z' makes it memorable, and it has the potential to be used in reality since zebra are social animals, usually living in small herds with one stallion and several females and their young. Because of the make-up of the group these herds are also sometimes referred to as harems. But 'a zeal of zebras' does attempt to stay true to the ethos of the original inventors of collective nouns in trying to convey something of the zebra's characteristics. The *OED* defines zeal as 'great energy or enthusiasm in pursuit of a cause or an objective', which is an accurate description of the fervour with which zebra will defend themselves and especially their young when under threat. If cornered by a predator an adult zebra will rear up on its hind legs and kick with its front legs to fend of its attacker. The animals have even been known to bite back at leopards and lions.

BIBLIOGRAPHY

Almond, Richard, *Medieval Hunting*, The History Press, 2012

Chalmers, Alexander (editor), *The Works of the English Poets from Chaucer to Cowper*, J. Johnson, 1810 (e-book digitized by Google)

Chaucer, Geoffrey, *The Canterbury Tales*, The Riverside Chaucer, Oxford University Press, 2008

Corner, Rachel, 'More Fifteenth-century "Terms of Association"', article in *The Review of English Studies*, Clarendon Press, 1962

Dryden, John, *Selected Poems*, Pearson Education Ltd, 2007

Fossier, Robert (editor), *The Cambridge Illustrated History of the Middle Ages: Volume III, 1250–1520*, Cambridge University Press, 1986

Hare, C. E., *The Language of Field Sports*, Country Life, 1939

Hentschell, Dr Roze, *The Culture of Cloth in Early Modern England: Textual Constructions of a National Identity*, Ashgate Press, 2008

Hodgkin, John, *Proper Terms: An Attempt at a Rational Explanation of the Meanings of the Collection of Phrases in 'The Book of St Albans', 1486, Entitled 'The Compaynys of Beestys and Fowlys' and Similar Lists*, Supplement to the Transactions of the Philological Society 1907-1910, Kegan, Paul, Trench & Trübner & Co. Ltd, London, 1909

Holmes, George, *The Oxford Illustrated History of Medieval Europe*, Oxford University Press, 2001

Kurath, Hans, *Middle English Dictionary, Volume 3*, The University of Michigan Press, 1959

Lipton, James, *An Exaltation of Larks: The Ultimate Edition*, Penguin Books, 1993

Lyon, Ann, *Constitutional History of the United Kingdom*, Routledge-Cavendish, 2003

Malory, Sir Thomas, *Le Morte d'Arthur: The Winchester Manuscript*, Oxford University Press, 1998

Maxwell, W. H., *The Field Book or Sports and Pastimes of the United Kingdom Compiled from Sources Ancient and Modern*, Effingham Wilson, 1833. Digitized at archive.org

Newman, Paul B., *Daily Life in the Middle Ages*, McFarland & Company Inc., 1961

Palin, Steve, *A Murmuration of Starlings: The Collective Nouns of Animals and Birds*, Merlin Unwin Books, 1993

Payne Collier, John (editor), *Old Ballads, From Early Printed Copies of the Utmost Rarity: Now for the First Time Collected*, Percy Society, 1840 (ebook edition)

The Penny Magazine of the Society for the Diffusion of Useful Knowledge, 1838

Phillips, Kim M., *Medieval Maidens: Young Women and Gender in England, 1270–1540*, Manchester University Press, 2003

Salgado, Gamini, *The Elizabethan Underworld*, The History Press, 1977

Shakespeare, William, *The Oxford Shakespeare: The Complete Works*, 2nd Edition, Oxford University Press, 2005

Shipley, Joseph Twadell, *The Origins of English Words: A Discursive Dictionary of Indo–European Roots*, John Hopkins University Press, 1984

The Sporting Magazine, or Monthly Calendar of the Transactions of the Turf, the Chace, etc, 1801

Thrupp, Sylvia L., *The Merchant Class of Medieval London, 1300–1500*, University of Chicago Press, 1948

Ward, Jennifer, *Women in England in the Middle Ages*, Hambledon Continuum, 2006

Woop Studios, *A Compendium of Collective Nouns: From an Armory of Aardvarks to a Zeal of Zebras*, Chronicle Books, 2013

Medieval sources:

Barnes, Dame Juliana, *The Book of St Albans* (*The Boke of Saint Albans: Containing Treatises on Hawking, Hunting, Cote-Armour, Fishing and Blasing of Arms*), 1486

Booke of Hawkyng after Prince Edwarde Kyng of Englande, a Manuscript of the Reign of Edward IV of England, British Library, Harley Collection 2340

Lydgate, John, 'Horse, Sheep, Goose' ('A Disputation between a Horse, a Sheepe and a Goose, for Superioritie'), printed by William Caxton, 1477

Tuberville, George, *The Book of Hunting*, 1575

ACKNOWLEDGEMENTS

Thanks to Heather Rhodes and John Rhodes, Annette Hibberd, Jim Hibberd and Matt Hibberd, Aubrey Smith for his beautiful illustrations, and to Louise Dixon, Lindsay Davies and the editorial and design team at Michael O'Mara Books, especially Claire Cater and Billy Waqar.

INDEX